The Shut-Out Wife

Breaking Through Your Husband's Midlife Crisis

Debra Macleod, B.A., J.D.
with Don Macleod

© 2022 Copyright Debra Macleod

Second Edition © 2024

Print edition: ISBN 978-1-990640-25-4
Ebook edition: ISBN 978-1-990640-28-5

All rights reserved. This book or any portion thereof may not be reproduced or used in any manner whatsoever without the express written permission of the author.

All people, correspondence, and situations presented in this book have been fictionalized, altered and/or generalized for illustration purposes: names, dialogue and identifying details do not represent actual persons and any resemblance to actual persons is purely coincidental. The author is not engaged in rendering professional advice or services to the individual reader. The relationship strategies presented herein are for general informational purposes and are based on the principles of effective communication, conflict resolution and positive interactions within marriage, as well as the author's experience as a relationship author and couples' mediator: they may not be suitable for all or serious marital problems. The author is not a mental health practitioner and this book is not appropriate in situations of mental illness or instability or abuse. The content herein is of a general nature only, and is not intended to be relied upon as, nor to be a substitute for, specific professional advice. Only the reader can judge the suitability of this book's content to his/her specific situation. If in doubt please consult a professional. The author cannot be held liable for any act or omission allegedly arising, directly or indirectly, from the use or misuse of this book.

Cover Photograph: Red heart in ice cubes on blue © Holmes Su. Shutterstock.com
Image on tablet: Sad woman sitting at edge of bed © Andrey Popov Shutterstock.com

DebraMacleod.com

TABLE OF CONTENTS

Introduction – Page 4

Topics covered: A shut-out wife, getting it right, my approach, how to proceed, from Don's desk, an overview of this book

Part One: How to Avoid or Downgrade His Midlife Crisis – Page 16

Topics covered: Why it's happened, how to prevent it from getting worse, dealing with his changing sex drive, managing his challenging behaviors, from Don's desk, how to make yourself more appealing to him, staying connected, reinforcing intimacy

Part Two: When His Midlife Episode Escalates – Page 70

Topics covered: The stages of a midlife crisis, dealing with his new interests or obsessions, managing his self-focus and even worse behaviors, from Don's desk, how to stay on track

Part Three: His "Friendships" With Other Women and Extramarital Affairs – Page 148

Topics covered: Other women and female friendships, when he won't end an affair, how to manage his infidelity, the shut-out wife's creed, how to make him want you again, from Don's desk

In Closing: The Meaning of (Mid)Life – Page 210

Topics covered: The 50/50, the part you're given, words of wisdom

Introduction

<u>Does Any of This Sound Familiar?</u>

Although every situation is unique, many wives see striking similarities when it comes to their husband's behavior during a so-called midlife crisis, specifically the type that involves a significant degree of self-focus and that puts a serious strain on the marriage, often to the brink—and unfortunately, sometimes beyond—of divorce and infidelity. In such cases, women often say they feel "shut out" out of their husband's lives.

They also report hearing the following expressions, or at least versions of them. Give these a read, and then ask yourself if any sound familiar to you:

"I love you, but I'm not in love with you."
"I don't know what I want."
"I feel like I'm missing out, and I want to experience everything."
"I don't know if I've ever been truly happy."
"Life is short, I have to live while I can."
"I can't live with anymore regrets."
"You've never really let me be my true self."
"I have to find out who I am...I need to live my own life for a while."
"I haven't been happy for a long time now."
"I need space. I'm confused..."

These kinds of statements, and a plethora of similar sentiments, can make your head spin. What is he talking about? There were so many good times, so many good things in your marriage. Yet no matter how many times you ask him what he means or how you can help, you just can't get a straight or meaningful answer.

He seems to be re-writing your history as a couple, erasing all the good stuff in the process.

A man's behavior during a midlife crisis or midlife episode can be equally confusing. He might be more emotional or getting in touch with his spiritual side. He might be looking for more meaning or adventure in life. Those can be good things, and in the best cases, he hasn't totally shut you out of this journey, at least not yet. If that's where you are, great. We'll work with that.

But things might not be or stay that positive. He may be profoundly self-focused. He may be making large purchases. He may start to act like an entitled adolescent instead of a devoted husband. He may become obsessed with fitness or another new activity and find a new group of friends, mostly female, spending more time with them, and less with you.

As he sends mixed messages, and becomes increasingly secretive and defensive, you may worry that he is on the brink of having an affair or that he's already having one. Those fears are often reasonable. Infidelity is common during a man's destructive and self-focused midlife crisis. Many wives have discovered their husband is sleeping with someone else, whether a younger woman or an old flame.

And soon after that, she can expect his behavior to become even more self-indulgent, mean-spirited or dismissive. He may act like your life together never existed as he moves out of your home to be with his girlfriend, and may even cut or limit contact with his own children.

You, meanwhile, may be reduced to pleading with him to come back, or desperately trying to assure him that things can get better. You spend all your time and energy analyzing him, diagnosing him, suggesting treatments, warning him that his kids will never forgive him or begging him to see a counselor or coach with you—and all for nothing, because he isn't listening.

And then you shake your head and say, **"He's completely shut me out. What should I do now?"**

You're Shut Out, or Close to It. Now What?

It may be that you've seen this crisis coming for months or even years. Or, maybe it's hit you out of the blue. It may be that you still have some connection and intimacy with your husband. Or, maybe he's shut you out completely, perhaps even moving out of the home. Perhaps he's having an emotional or physical affair, or you feel he may soon have one.

Regardless, you've been put into an emotional tailspin. How could this person, to whom you've given so many years and with whom you've shared so much, now treat you with such indifference or disrespect?

You find yourself living in a constant state of uncertainty, hurt and anxiety. You're confused, but mostly you're afraid. Afraid to be alone, afraid to lose this man you love, your history, the life and family you've built over the years.

You're afraid that you're powerless to stop what is happening—but you're not. That's because you're here, reading this.

A man's midlife crisis can be an unpredictable thing and you need to be prepared. You need to be a mini-expert in what he might do and why, in what he's thinking and feeling, and how he may interpret and react to the things you say and do in response to him.

You need to decode his behavior and make him see you with fresh eyes—and also see that he can't keep doing what he's doing. You need to turn this situation around, so that he's the one who's afraid of losing you. You need to stabilize and then strengthen your marriage so that it can be a sanctuary of love, intimacy and devoted companionship for both of you.

So take a deep breath. You may be in tears, you may be furious, you may be panicked or confused, but you can get through this. Right now, you need to realize that you're at a crossroads in your marriage and life.

At this pivotal time, you cannot let your fear or anger or sadness, or your husband's baffling or self-focused behavior, get the better of you.

Right now, you need to start saying and doing the things that are in your best interests, and in the best interests of your marriage, and you need to do this despite the whirlwind of emotion and uncertainty swirling around you.

The Importance of Getting It Right – Right Now

A husband's midlife crisis can be one of the greatest threats to a woman's emotional well-being in mid and later life. I'm saddened when I see a woman faced with this, especially at a time that should be stable and carefree, when she should be enjoying happy, loving companionship with her husband.

I'm also frustrated, because it seems that women are getting a lot of bad advice. They are often advised to simply wait out their husband's midlife crisis, or to provide unconditional wifely support, as if the turmoil they are experiencing is subordinate to his.

Sometimes, they're even encouraged to play some kind of game to win him back, or to compromise their own dignity. *"Be sexier...and whatever you do, do NOT complain about anything!"* Or perhaps they're encouraged to play tough. *"Stop taking his calls—that'll show him!"*

Now, to be sure, there are times when these snippets of advice are golden. The challenge lies in understanding whether and when to actually use them (or something similar to them), so that your efforts don't either fall flat or backfire altogether.

Because every time you try something and it doesn't work, the actual solution gets a little further away. That's why you need to start reading this book right now, cover to cover, before you inadvertently make matters worse. It's time to think, to absorb some new insights and strategies, and to try something different.

Too often, a woman who is faced with a husband's midlife crisis is so eager to regain his love and her sense of security that she will just carpet-bomb solutions, throwing everything out there, and often missing the target altogether. There's no method to the madness, so to speak.

At the same time, a woman who faces this crisis can be quite stubborn, sometimes without even realizing it. If someone gives her a useful bit of advice, she dismisses it. *"No, that's not the problem."* Or, *"I've already tried that, it didn't work."*

Quite often, she has a preconceived idea of the advice she wants to hear, or what the problem is, and she isn't willing to go down any path but that one (and incidentally, this is why some practitioners simply tell a woman in this situation what she wants to hear—it makes their job easier).

Of course, there is some merit in this woman's thinking— after all, no one knows a husband better than his wife. Yet, too often, it is that very familiarity that can obscure the problem. It's just too close for a woman to see it clearly.

There's simply too much assumption and emotion, and too little objectivity and recasting. There's far too much presumption and empty speculation, and not enough open-minded experimentation.

My Approach and the Evolution of *The Shut-Out Wife*

After law school, I worked for some time as a divorce mediator. During those years, I saw many couples divorce, but the ones that surprised me the most were couples who divorced in mid or later life. I always privately thought, *You've made it this far, why now? You've raised your kids, paid off your house—why would you go your separate ways now?* It just didn't make sense.

It was only after I shifted the focus of my practice from divorce mediation to couples' / marital mediation—a style of mediation designed **to help people stay together and keep their marriages intact**—that I came to understand this phenomenon in a real-world way, from the perspective of both the shut-out wife and those husbands who, after their midlife episode had ended, wished to reconcile with their estranged wife.

This became one of my areas of practice, and I eventually arranged my best insights and strategies into resources that more people could access, summing up the experiences of countless wives and husbands, so that women in particular could know that they weren't alone and that there is a way to manage this marriage crisis in an effective and dignified way. The content in this book is therefore tested and true, since I've only included material that has worked for my clients.

Like any crisis a woman faces in her life (and we've all faced a few, haven't we?), this one must be managed rationally, creatively and assertively. Simply hoping for the best isn't a strategy. It's the absence of a strategy. And too often, while a wife is hoping for the best and being supportive, her husband's behavior continues to escalate.

He continues to focus only on himself, to re-write their history, to criticize her or blame her for his unhappiness, and to recreate himself as a more youthful, exciting and physically fit man. And when the New Him is complete, to hook up with a younger woman he met at spin class. So, that's what he's often doing while his supportive wife is hoping for the best.

Does that sound like too much attitude? Too bad. You're going to need some attitude to deal with this.

Of course you need to support your husband if he is experiencing a midlife episode, and you'll find ways here to do that. Your marriage must be happy and fulfilling for both of you, and there are ways to get through this together. There are also resources out there to help a man in a midlife crisis, if he will use them.

But when he refuses to take that initiative, and when his crisis creates a crisis in your life and marriage, you can't just wait it out. You need an inventory of usable information, of practical "do this, don't do that" strategies to draw from.

You need to know how to handle yourself, what to say and what to do when you're caught off-guard by his behavior, and how to counteract the things he's saying and doing, so that you can limit the damage to your marriage.

You need to understand, respect and be fair to what he's going through. You need to understand your role in things. Yet very importantly, you also need to be aware of any possible manipulations on your spouse's part, and be ready and able to deal with those. Because there are *some* people who may use a midlife episode as an excuse to indulge in certain behaviors. Self-determination on your part is therefore essential.

Striking that balance—being fair to him, but aware of challenging behaviors and possible manipulations, and knowing how to manage those—is the basis of my "Fair, but Aware" approach, one that stems from my training and experience. After all, mediation and legal training teach you to see both sides of a situation—or indeed, the many sides. That's what I'll pass on to you. You need to see what's happening from multiple angles and perspectives.

Yet when it comes to marital relationships, an approach like this needs to have a certain softness, inventiveness and flexibility so that it can take into account the feelings and circumstances that accompany marital problems. It also needs to go beyond resolving the specific problem (i.e. a midlife episode) to actually enhance feelings of love, intimacy and devotion.

In my opinion, that requires a practitioner with personal as well as professional experience with marriage. At the time of writing this book, my husband Don and I have been married for over twenty years. We have been writing and collaborating for as long, and have consulted with many couples and spouses, including shut-out wives, and husbands who are experiencing a midlife episode.

That's another reason why the insights and strategies you'll read herein are realistic and balanced. We've dealt with both sides, had frank conversations with both wives and husbands, and followed the types of behaviors—and responses—that tend to happen, thus learning what tends to make things better and what tends to make things worse. As a relationship author who has done his own fair share of research and work with couples, and as a man who's been married long enough to have experienced the ups and downs of married and family life, you'll receive the benefit of Don's perspective in everything I write herein, and sometimes in his own words.

So that's a look at my approach. But as with any approach, it is not the only one out there, and it is not right for every person or every situation— you have options, from mental health professionals to lawyers, depending on your preferences and needs. In my opinion, no matter how many people call themselves marriage or relationship experts, you are the true expert in your marriage. I'm a big believer that people who are otherwise healthy and functional can improve their own situations once they have an inventory of usable insights and strategies to draw from; however, things can change. So stay proactive and always get the type of help you need.

In this book, I truly want to help you manage your husband and the gut-wrenching, soul-sucking situation of feeling shut out of his life as the self-indulgent aspects of his midlife crisis take over and threaten to destroy your marriage.

As a shut-out wife, you haven't just been dealing with your husband's behavior. You've been struggling with your own fears and feelings, perhaps even questioning your own worth and desirability. You want nothing more than for him to come to his senses, to reassure you that you're the only woman in the world he could ever love. You'd do anything for him to come to you and apologize, to feel adored by him and secure in your marriage, and for the two of you to recommit to spending the rest of your life together.

Now let's pause there for a moment—the rest of your life. That's what this book is really all about. It's about you taking back your life and having a say in your own future. It's about using strategies that have the best chance of motivating your husband to recommit to your shared life in a loving and respectful way—if that's what you decide you want. No more living in a constant state of uncertainty, fear, anxiety or heartache.

No more living in the wake of your husband's behavior, stuck in a cycle of hope and disappointment.

You have options. You always have, and you always will. You've just become so confused and emotional that you may have forgotten.

How to Proceed and a General Overview of Contents

So—let's look at how this book actually works. As you'll see, I've divided it into three parts. Because my approach is designed to help women address this problem in a logical, structured and guided way, it's important that you read all parts, in order.

Every word has the potential to be relevant, even crucial to you at some point. Even if you don't think a certain part applies to you, and even if you'd rather go directly to the part that you feel is most relevant, you should read in order. Many of the strategies I offer are cumulative, and I'll be referencing and building upon them as we move through each part.

Earlier, I said a woman who is faced with this issue can be stubborn, and that she might have preconceived ideas of what is going on and/or how to improve things. This is where you prove me wrong by reading everything, in order, and keeping an open mind while you do.

Because if you knew what was wrong and how to fix it, you wouldn't be reading this. So put in the time and do it right. Read everything. Think about everything. Then—and only then—decide what you are going to accept and implement, and what you are not. Worst case, you lose a few hours. Best case, you see something from a new angle.

Let's move on now to take a look at the three parts of this book.

In part one, I'll help you avoid or downgrade a midlife crisis so it isn't a crisis at all, but rather a life transition that can make your marriage happier and more stable for both of you. I'll address some of the most common problems that can arise so that you can tackle those before they become major issues (or at least come back to them if it's work you haven't done yet). The goal here is to keep you connected as a loving, devoted couple.

In part two, I'll walk you through the typical stages of a midlife crisis so you can that big picture view. I'll then jump right into the trenches with you and help you manage those midlife situations that have escalated. I'll talk about how to cope with his fitness obsession, or other new focuses, and what to do when the "new him" comes with an inflated ego. I'll help you navigate his self-focus, negativity or criticism of you.

I'll also cover those higher-conflict, confusing behaviors—when he seems uncertain about the marriage or doesn't know what he wants, when he sends mixed messages, when he's mean or moody, and when he says things like "I love you but I'm not in love with you."

In part three, we'll focus on midlife crises and extramarital affairs. It's common for men experiencing a serious midlife crisis to find validation and excitement by befriending younger women, and this often leads to affairs. I'll talk about how you should handle his friendships with other women, especially those friendships he is particularly protective of or that you feel have crossed the line.

Of all the scenarios a wife can face, this is obviously the most confusing and painful. You need to understand what's happening and you need to be careful in terms of what you say and do. If he's having an affair, you'll find material here that can help you reclaim your dignity, power (and by power, I mean personal power or personal empowerment) and sense of control over your own marriage and life. You'll also find insights and strategies that can motivate him to end an affair and recommit to the life you share, if that is what you want to happen.

Throughout the book, I'll be putting various strategies and insights into context for you by walking you through mini case-scenarios. This is so you can actually visualize yourself using these approaches in your marriage in a very real-world way. I'll show you how some of my strategies have worked for previous clients—women *and* men.

That's because, in the end, the goal here isn't just to make you happy—it's to make your husband happy, too. It's to bring the two of you back together and to rebuild your marriage on the foundation of a loving partnership.

I've spoken to many men over the years who came out the other side of a destructive midlife crisis after doing serious damage to their marriage, and who deeply regretted the fallout it created in their own life, and in the lives of their wife and children.

So yes, this book is for women, but the goal is to help men, too. We're in it together.

Which leads me to another point. It may be your husband who is behaving in overtly destructive ways, but that doesn't mean I'm not going to ask you to take an honest look at your own behavior or shortcomings in the marriage.

Just like you, your husband may have legitimate complaints about you or life you share—we need to look at those, and we need to make sure the dynamics between you are really positive. And yes, there is always room for improvement.

Yet whether he's being sincere or not, you need to break down what is happening and handle it smartly. You can do that by tailoring this book's content to your situation. I've included some Q&A's—questions for you to ask yourself and thoughtfully answer—at the end of parts one, two and three. These are great for review, but even better to help you focus and put the material to use.

So... find a space to read, whether it's at your desk during your lunchbreak or curled up on your couch at home. Better yet, go for a change of scenery—go sit on a park bench somewhere and read, or even go stay at a friend's for a couple nights. Get away from it all for a while, and put some physical space between you and the situation. That can help you see your situation at a lot more clearly. It can help you process a book like this a lot more clearly, too. Perspective is so important.

Now, let's turn the page, literally and figuratively, and get to work.

Part One:

How to Avoid or Downgrade His Midlife Crisis

The "Why's" of a Man's Midlife Crisis

Let's start with a question you've asked yourself a thousand times: "Why is my husband acting like this?" I'm going to run through some reasons here; however, I'm not going to spend much time on this. This book is not an exhaustive study into why some men have so-called midlife crises. In fact, there is no consensus that the midlife crisis is actually real *per se*. We may see a set of similar emotions and behaviors in our culture when a person reaches a certain age, and we label those a midlife crisis, but it isn't a diagnosis. Rather, it's a natural experience, a transition, that attends aging for men and women alike—albeit one that some people experience in more negative and extreme ways than others.

Therefore, this book is focused on helping you as a shut-out wife manage what is happening in a sensible, practical way. That means less theoretical speculation and more real-world information and ideas. The insights and strategies I share in this book come directly from my experience working with spouses who have gone through these more negative and extreme midlife crises. I only share with you the information that reflects real struggles and outcomes.

So back to it. Why might your husband be having a midlife crisis or showing related behaviors and attitudes? The most obvious reason is that he's started to notice the physical changes associated with getting older. I've felt them, you've felt them and your husband feels them. He's well aware of his changing appearance and likely his diminishing energy level. He may be having some performance issues in terms of sex. Even if he isn't, he's probably worried that's going to happen at some point.

Being self-conscious about his body and performance can make any man question his virility and desirability, and he may start to seek outside reassurance that he still has plenty of both. I don't say this in a derogatory way. Everyone wants to feel desirable and youthful. The beauty industry rakes in billions every year by tapping into the female longing to be desirable, doesn't it?

Yet aging isn't just a physical process. It's an emotional one, too. It makes the best of us ask questions about choices we've made. We have regrets and disappointments and unfortunately those have a way of overshadowing the joys and the accomplishments.

If a person hasn't achieved everything they wanted to in life, they may be fearful that their time has passed or they're out of time. They may look at the person or people closest to them, such as their spouse and even their kids, and secretly resent the sacrifices they've had to make (or feel they've had to make) for them. This way of thinking—especially if it becomes habitual and entrenched—can make a person forget about all the good things their spouse and kids have brought into their life.

At the same time, a person who has met with the kind of success they were hoping for in life might also experience a midlife crisis. They may realize that success isn't as fulfilling as they thought it would be. They may have a sense of, "What, is that all?"

Middle age can also bring a sense of deeper regret. Most people have some level of regret as they reach middle age: *"I should've done this instead of that."* Much of this is speculative: *"I wonder what would've happened if I'd done this instead of that?"*

Most of us come to terms with this. We accept and realize that there will always be unanswered questions. No one can travel down every road life has to offer. There just isn't enough time. Instead, we accept, with maturity and perspective, the gifts that life has given us. But other people have more serious regrets, the kind that they struggle to come to terms with. The kind that haunts them and makes it hard to find peace.

Boredom is another thing that drives some midlife crisis behavior. By the time most of us reach middle age, the kids are either grown and gone, or grown enough that they don't need as much of our time and energy as they used to. They're living their own lives, and we're free to live ours.

Yet in some cases, we're so accustomed to family life, and to all the demands that has put on us over the years, that we don't know what to do with ourselves when those demands are fewer!

In our younger years, life was full of new things— marriage, family, and career. But by the time many people reach middle age, those new experiences—life's big ones—are often behind us. Now we're watching our kids experience those things while we are facing retirement.

Not everyone accepts that or adapts to that with the grace and gratitude they should. There are positive ways to channel that boredom and to get excited about life again, to experience a sense of youthful adventure and a fresh start—and we'll get to that—but unfortunately not everyone does that. Some men who display midlife crisis behavior handle "boredom" and the aging process in the worst ways possible.

Panic is another strong emotion that fuels midlife crisis behavior. The feeling that time is running out and that we're going to miss out. That we're not tasting everything life can dish up. That other people are getting more out of their life, while we're just sitting here, doing the same thing day after day, while life passes us by, and evermore quickly.

But perhaps the biggest and most encompassing emotion that attends aging is fear. Getting older is scary. The idea of dying is scary. Picture the Grim Reaper—he's not wearing Bermuda shorts and holding an umbrella drink, is he? No, he's wearing an ominous black robe and carrying a sickle.

Age makes us keenly aware of own mortality and this kind of fear can certainly drive a person to behave in some uncharacteristic ways. In fact, you could argue that everything I've talked about to this point—the self-consciousness about physical changes, the regret, the desire for a new adventure, the panic—they all come from a place of fear.

I've seen some men embark on a midlife crisis after the death of a parent or close friend. That hits really close to home and makes it real. And that's really scary.

* * * * * * *

FROM DON'S DESK

Most of the reasons that Debra mentioned have to do with a husband on a personal level, and how he feels about himself and his own life. As a man who is in his midlife years at the time of writing this book, I can confirm they're all spot on. The male ego is a real thing. It's not evil or awful, at least it doesn't have to be, but it is real and middle age can knock the hell out of it.

Things like performance issues, hair loss, and how we don't look quite so good in a tee-shirt anymore, cut deep. Like Debra said, I'm sure you can identify with these insecurities.

But sometimes, relationship issues can contribute to what he's feeling and what you're seeing as well.

Are you in serious debt or do you argue about how to spend your money? Do you disagree on how to socialize or spend your time? Have you put your marriage and sex life on the back-burner while you were raising your kids or saving up for retirement?

Is your marriage burdened with negativity or hard-feelings or silent resentments? Do you struggle to communicate or stay close, or have you said some nasty things to each other? Trust me, he'll remember.

Eventually, this book will look at how your relationship may be factoring into your husband's midlife episode. Because whether or not you have marriage problems, it's very common for men who are having a midlife crisis to point to their marriage and wife and say, "It's not me, that's the problem!"

And the more he thinks this way, the more he thinks this way. Eventually his attitude begins to reflect this way of thinking. So you need to address any relationship issues, or rule them out, as the case may be. Regardless, for now, just tuck this away for deeper thought later.

* * * * * * *

In the end, the reasons for a midlife episode often overlap. A man might be noticing a decrease in energy level combined with feelings of fear and regret, and the death of a close friend. So, when I talk about the reasons for a midlife, I'm not suggesting that there is going to be one prevailing reason. There might be, but it's more likely going to be a number of things. Some may have merit, others none, but they all have to be understood and dealt with.

Let's return now to that big question. Why is this happening? I hope you can answer that now, at least to some extent.

But What About Your Midlife Crisis as a Woman?

I'm often asked if women also experience midlife crises (or at least the feelings and behaviors we associate with that concept) and the answer is a resounding *yes*. Some women go through precisely the same kind of midlife crises that I talk about in this book, including the really nasty ones.

By that, I mean the ones that include saying hurtful things to their spouse, having affairs and basically walking away from the marriage and family they've spent a lifetime with. The ones that are fueled by fear, regret, or boredom, and that are characterized by self-focus and self-indulgence.

Why do I mention this? Well, because I don't want to imply that only men do this. Trust me, women can be every bit as self-focused and mean-spirited as men can be. They can make all the same mistakes. Yet the fact remains, in my practice, I speak with a disproportionate number of women who are struggling to cope with a husband's midlife crisis. That's why I wrote this book specifically for women.

I've found that many women experience midlife in a different, very female way. And this has less to do with fear and more to do with freedom.

I've found that many women who leave their marriages in middle age were unhappy in those marriages for a long time. Many stayed because of finances and especially because of their kids. But once their children had left home, they realized they had the freedom to leave. And they embraced that freedom.

Other women, women in happier or more stable marriages, also embrace the freedom that midlife can bring. The freedom from having to be there 24/7 for their children or their boss or whatever.

The freedom of finally not caring what other people think. The freedom of being able to be themselves and to know that those they love will always be there for them.

This concept of freedom is an important one. When many women reach middle age, they want to feel that way—free! Free from the anxiety, uncertainty and insecurity that many of us have had to deal with in life.

Yet if you're coping with a husband who's going through a midlife crisis, especially one of the nastier kinds, that kind of freedom is hard to come by. Instead of feeling comforted and confident in your marriage at this point in your life, you feel the exact opposite. You feel imprisoned by anxiety, uncertainty and insecurity. And that has to change.

As we move through this book, remember that another one of your goals is to break free from that anxiety, uncertainty and insecurity. You can't simply live as a slave to your husband's whims and words and actions. You need to break free from that. You need to have emotional and mental freedom.

Because that freedom is the gift of age, and you have every right to accept it. You've earned it.

How to Make It Better Instead of Worse

Earlier, I went through the possible reasons for a midlife episode. I talked about the self-consciousness that comes with body changes, as well as the regret, the desire for a new adventure, and the panic and fear. Don talked a bit about the possibility of underlying marital issues.

These are all things that I would hope and expect you are able to empathize with. Because if your husband is showing signs of a midlife crisis and beginning to say things or behave in ways that are out of character, one of the most important things you can do to prevent it from escalating is to empathize with whatever emotions are behind those words and behaviors.

It's helpful to ask yourself some probing questions. What might my husband be feeling? What might he be unhappy with or feeling insecure about? What might he be fearful of as he ages?

Once you know the answers to those kinds of questions, or at least have a good idea based on your knowledge of him—or once you're simply more sensitive to those kinds of questions and willing to explore them—you can show empathy for his thoughts and emotions. That, in itself, can make things better.

Unfortunately, a lot of wives don't do this. They don't put serious thought into what's triggering their husband's words or behaviors, and they don't show empathy for what he's feeling and thinking. Instead, they dismiss or even ridicule what he's experiencing. They might respond critically or coldly.

(Are you doing this? Probably not. But keep reading anyway…just in case. If nothing else, it's a friendly reminder.)

For example, if their husband wants to get his motorbike license, they might say, "Why do you want to ride a motorbike? You're fifty-five. You're too old." If their husband wants to get in better shape and run a marathon, they might say, "What's the point at your age?"

My point is this: instead of recognizing their husband's new ideas or uncharacteristic behaviors for what they are—the actions of someone trying to cope with midlife issues and fears—they dismiss them and make their husband turn even more inward. Trust me, this is not the kind of rejection a middle-aged man wants to experience. This is not the smartest time in a woman's life for her to reject her husband's changing ideas and interests. It will only make things worse.

Instead, I encourage wives to support these kinds of harmless or positive re-inventions of the self, and to show excitement and interest in what he's proposing. If he says he wants to get his motorbike license or get in better shape, why not? If he wants to start volunteering or become a more spiritual person, why not? If he wants to travel to an unusual place, somewhere that's off the map for the two of you, why not? Like the old saying goes, if you can't beat 'em, join 'em.

Another way that some wives inadvertently make the situation worse is by saying things like, "Why do you want to spend your weekend parasailing? Don't you want to visit the kids instead?"

That is, they send their husband the message that he should be content with their current way of doing things and spending their time, and they may even try to guilt him into sticking with the status quo.

But it's a mistake to send a husband the message that his life is "good enough" and that he shouldn't want to make any changes or try new things.

Of course, there are certain things that he must be content with and deeply grateful for—your marriage and your children are obviously at the top of that list. And as we move through this book, we'll do what we can to make sure he clearly recognizes that, and that you stay at the top of that list. But that doesn't mean he has to be content with *everything*.

That doesn't mean you can't break the status quo a bit. Remember I talked about freedom? At this time in your life, you may have the freedom to do what you want to do, instead of just what you have to do. So get on board with that.

Push your own boundaries and don't be afraid to venture outside your own comfort zone. Give yourself a kick in your own complacency. Not only can this make your own life more interesting, it creates an essential, all-important dynamic—it makes midlife about the two of you, as a married couple, as a team. It makes the journey about the both of you, instead of just about your husband.

As you'll see in this book, and as you may already know all too well, a man who is going through a midlife crisis can be a very self-focused, self-absorbed person. Therefore, the more you can do to make this journey about the both of you, instead of just him, the better off you'll be.

If you think about it, I'm sure that you've had some of the same thoughts and feelings that your husband has. Body image issues, a few regrets, a longing for new experiences, a sense that time is moving too fast and the sadness and fear that comes with that.

So empathize. Show your husband that you're experiencing midlife in your own way, that you understand what he's going through and that you want to have the kind of marriage where you support each other through this.

And just something to keep in mind here, and throughout this experience: if you ever feel like your husband is becoming depressed or overly anxious, or having trouble coping in a more serious way, you should recommend that he see a mental health professional (that goes for you, too, by the way!). Because many men are reluctant to seek counseling, you can help by putting a positive spin on it. Let him know that it's the strongest, most capable people who are proactive about their well-being, and that he definitely falls into that category. Let him know that he's been there for you and your kids, and now it's time for him to be there for himself.

How to Deal With His Declining Sex Drive or Performance

Now, there's something else I want to mention here because it's one of the main ways that a wife inadvertently makes things worse. And it has to do with your husband's sexual performance. It's common for men in middle age to notice some changes: they may find it more difficult to get or sustain an erection.

When this happens to a man, his wife might say something like, "It doesn't matter, I'm happy just being close." Or, she might suggest that he see his doctor, since there is medicine that may be able to help. In some cases, his wife may experience frustration. She might say something like, "Why aren't you doing anything about this?"

I get that your husband's changing sexual drive or performance affects you: it may make you frustrated, it may make you feel bad for him, it may make you worried about the future of your marriage as the sexual intimacy between you begins to wane. So it's understandable that you want to suggest ideas to help matters.

After all, that's what we do as women. We fix things. We take the initiative and do some investigating and then we make things better. Many of us have spent decades doing this at work and at home.

But this head-on approach is often the wrong approach when it comes to this very sensitive issue, and I'll tell you why. It's unnecessary. Believe me, your husband is fully aware of the changes that are happening to him. He is keenly aware of it—in fact, he was aware it was happening long before you became aware of it. So there's no need for you to bring it to his attention or initiate a conversation about it.

You're well aware of changes to your own body, right? And you'd prefer to address those in your own way and in your own time, right? Well, the same holds true with your husband. He knows what is happening and he knows he can book an appointment with his doctor to have it investigated. You don't need to do that for him.

A head-on approach with respect to this issue can also be counter-productive. Pointing it out or saying that it doesn't matter just shines the spotlight on what's happening. That can make an already self-conscious man even more self-conscious.

Instead, I often suggest to my clients that they focus on their own pleasure and especially on showing their husband that he can still pleasure them.

If you're in bed being intimate and he's unable to perform, don't miss a beat—move his hands down to pleasure you. Show him that he can excite you and satisfy you. Let him feel that sense of power and capability. Flatter him. Stroke his ego. Don't go overboard or make it phony. Keep it sweet, simple and sincere.

Your husband knows it's happening. He knows that you know it's happening. He knows he can see his doctor about it. So handle this issue with compassion and grace. Show him that you desire him and that he has the power to satisfy you. Leave the rest to him.

It's important for you to realize that one of the main things that cause a midlife to escalate is a man's fear that his sex drive and his sexual ability are declining. That can prompt him to basically prove to himself that he's still got it. And unfortunately many men who are going through midlife will prove this to themselves by seeking validation from other women, often younger women.

You can reduce the risk of this happening by being the woman who validates him, both in and out of the bedroom. By singing his praises and making him feel desired, by making him feel good about himself sexually, you can help make other women unnecessary. It isn't a guarantee—affairs can happen even if you do this—but it's a good step to take anyway.

(And just for the record, I'm still talking about situations that have not escalated to the point of egotism or an affair.)

When He Starts to Re-Write Your History as a Couple

Men who are experiencing a midlife crisis can become very self-focused. This can happen even if a man is having a fairly mild or minor midlife crisis.

That's why learning how to handle this self-focus is one of the first and one of the most important things you can do if you feel your husband is having a midlife crisis. It's an absolutely essential skill.

In the best of circumstances, you'll see this self-focus sneaking up on you and you'll be able to manage it early, before it gets worse. The more his midlife crisis escalates, the more his self-focus will likely escalate. The two go hand in hand.

You may notice an increasing self-focus in any number of ways. He may begin to be more distant or critical of you. He may begin to do more things by himself. He may begin to express his own unhappiness or how he feels unfulfilled in life. He may begin a new health and fitness regime, often a fairly obsessive one.

He may begin to re-write your history as a couple. By this, I mean that he begins to talk about your past in a more negative light. He seems to forget about the good times and focuses only on the bad times, often exaggerating how bad they really were.

He may begin to question things about his life or your life together. He may start to wonder whether you got married too young or whether you got married for the wrong reasons. He may start to second-guess decisions you made together, including career choices or where you chose to live.

He may start to look back at the marriage or family life and talk about all the sacrifices he made for them. He may bring up issues from the past, whether marital problems or financial mistakes, and talk about how he regrets those or how those have cost him the life he wanted.

When this starts to happen, most wives react in a knee-jerk way. They either get angry and defensive and start to argue, or they go into a sort of panic mode and start to apologize for everything, perhaps trying to persuade him that he isn't seeing the past or the situation clearly. They might talk about all the good times they've had and desperately try to get him to remember or acknowledge those.

Yet it's unlikely that either of these approaches is going to work. Why not? Because both allow him to remain self-focused. In fact, I'd say that both of these approaches actually make him more self-focused.

It's like this. If you simply get mad and start challenging him—*How can you say our life or marriage hasn't made you happy? You've always been happy!*—if you do this, you're only going to trigger a defensive response, one that makes him even more entrenched in his way of thinking. He'll dig in his heels.

He'll defend his position—that he hasn't been happy or that past mistakes haven't been laid to rest—and that'll make him even more certain that he's right. He will focus more on himself and his position, and less on you or the marriage.

At the same time, if you try to persuade him that he's wrong—*Think about all the times you have been happy! You're only remembering the bad times!*—if you do this, again, you're only going to trigger a defensive response as he resists what you're saying and tries to prove you wrong. He'll dig in his heels.

On top of that, you're setting a dangerous precedent. You're making it all about *his* happiness, *his* fulfillment, *his* way of seeing or remembering things. Again, this lets him focus more on himself and his position, and less on you or the marriage.

I suggest a different approach.

Instead of arguing or getting mad, instead of trying to persuade him to see things more clearly or in a more balanced way, shrug it off. Don't get into a debate.

Instead, let him feel heard, but state your truth. State it clearly and simply. It might sound something like this:

"I hear you, but I don't entirely agree. Hindsight is 20/20 and there are things I'd do differently as well. But I'm not going to look back and focus only or mostly on the bad. I'd rather focus on the future and making it better. I'd rather use the bad parts of our past as a learning experience, and as motivation to make the future a happier one for both of us."

This approach has a few benefits to it. First, it isn't all about him. Instead of just talking about his regrets or grievances, you're letting him know that *you* might have a few of your own. He still feels acknowledged and heard (which is always essential), but now you have a voice, too.

The fact is, some men who become self-focused during a midlife crisis completely lose sight of the fact that their wife might have her own reasons for being unhappy, or might have her own perspective on their marriage and past. They can become so wrapped up in their own feelings and thoughts that they completely forget their wife has her own. It just doesn't occur to them.

And the less it occurs to them, the more they focus only on themselves. So make sure it occurs to him. Don't let your panic and fear put you in a position where you make it all about him. That will backfire.

The second benefit of this approach is that it focuses on a positive future instead of a negative past. Many men who have midlife crises tend to focus on the past. They'll often re-write your past to suit their narrative. By making it seem worse than it was, they can justify or rationalize their current self-focused behavior. So try to adjust the focus to the future when you can.

The third benefit of this approach is that it envisions a *shared* happy future. You're finding common ground—your mutual desire for a happy and fulfilling relationship in middle age and beyond—and you're using that as a way to create a sense of solidarity between you.

You can think of this as the "aim and refocus" approach.

Aim toward a positive future, not the negative past. And then refocus the conversation from just being about him to being about you as well, and to one that presents you as a united couple going through life together.

But keep in mind that you must strike a balance, here. On one hand, you don't want him to become entirely self-focused. On the other hand, you don't want to dismiss him or make everything about your marriage or the two of you.

He needs to know that his individual needs, opinions and desires are important to you. It's a question of balance and respect, really. Listen to him, show empathy and caring for his position, but resist the urge to argue or persuade him that he's wrong. After all, this isn't about facts—it's about his feelings. You won't win this kind of argument. So try to avoid triggering that defensive response where you and he basically lock horns and dig in your heels, each trying to prove that you're right, and the other person is wrong. That dynamic only makes things worse.

Remember: the more a person feels compelled to defend their position, the more they often start to believe their position. We can all convince ourselves of something, so don't act in ways that will only push him further down that thought path.

State your truth. State it clearly and simply. You can use the "*I hear you, but I don't entirely agree...*" statement I gave earlier, although I suggest you think about your own statement, one that sounds more natural and like you. Speak from the heart, but speak with confidence. Don't obsess too much about the words you use. Instead, focus on the message and the vibe you want to send.

You want to send the message that you hear what he's saying and you care, but that you don't see it the same way. You want to send the message that you're acknowledging the past wasn't perfect, but it wasn't all bad either, and that you want your future to be happy for both of you.

Aim and re-focus. Aim toward a positive future. Refocus the dialogue from being all about him to being about the two of you. Do this with empathy and respect—respect for him and respect for yourself.

When He Starts to Blame You For His Unhappiness

It is fairly common for a man who is experiencing a midlife crisis, and who is becoming increasingly self-focused in the process, to begin to blame his wife for his own unhappiness. He may point to his wife and say, "*You're the reason I wasn't able to achieve my goals*" or "*You've never really been there for me*" or some kind of variation of this.

He may blame his wife for any and all marriage problems. "*You spent too much money. You weren't sexual or supportive enough. You never wanted to try new things.*"

He may also begin to moralize. That is, he ˙ message that he is more active or interested in life than his ͺ that he is more enlightened. The insinuation, of course, is thaͺ wife has held him back somehow. He may also insinuate that he has made all kinds of unappreciated or unrecognized sacrifices for the marriage or family unit, and that he has suffered in silence.

His message might be, "*I tried to tell you I wasn't happy but you didn't listen*" or "*I never said anything because I was too busy fulfilling my obligations and you were too focused on the kids.*" Something along those lines anyway. By doing this, he can explain away the fact that he didn't tell you earlier how unhappy he really was. So again, it's your fault.

I guess in some ways this is to be expected. After all, it's human nature to lash out at the person closest to us and to find blame there. That happens in many marriages, including those where midlife crises aren't an issue. It isn't fair, but it happens.

Now, I mentioned previously that some men re-write their history to be worse than it was so that they can justify their behavior. Some are very aware they're doing this and are doing it purposefully. But others are less aware. We can all get caught up in our thoughts, and those thoughts can get away from us.

It's the same thing with blame. If a husband can attribute the marriage problems and failures to his wife, then he has a good excuse to behave in the ways he is now behaving without feeling too guilty or badly about it. He has a good excuse to be cold or mean, or even to cheat or leave the marriage. He has a reason he can hold out to the world. It makes him feel entitled to his own self-focus and self-indulgence.

If you feel that your husband is starting to blame you for his unhappiness, if he's trying to blame you alone for any past issues or problems in the marriage and isn't acknowledging his own part in that, I want you to recognize that for what it may be—an attempt to pin it on you, so that he can start to view you as the bad guy and himself as the mistreated man.

If he can do this, he can obtain a license to do whatever he wants, and then claim that he's justified in doing it.

This is not a road you want to go down. This is not a dynamic or a habit that you want to let happen in your marriage. This is not a way of thinking or behaving that you want him to get used to. You need to stop it before it gets out of hand.

When this starts to happen, a woman typically reacts in either one of two very general ways, and they are similar to the ways she may react when confronted with him re-writing their history.

First, she may panic and begin to accept blame for everything, perhaps asking her husband what she can do to make up for it and make things better. She may say *"You're right, it was my fault! Please don't go—just tell me what you want me to do!"*

The second way she may react is by getting angry. She may say, *"Well you were to blame, too!"*

Although I can understand both reactions, it's unlikely that either one is going to work. Why not? Because taking blame for everything means that he can blame you for everything! It sets a bad precedent and you lose any power you had. And, frankly, it just isn't fair. It's unlikely you were to blame for everything that was wrong with the marriage.

Of course there were things you did wrong and could've done better, but that goes for both of you. So don't let the panic of his increasing distance or self-focus back you into a corner where you feel, out of desperation, that you have to take it all on yourself.

At the same time, getting mad and defensive and basically throwing accusations back at your husband won't work either. It's more likely that you'll trigger an even more determined, angry, or defensive reaction from him. And then the game's *really* on—it's a back-and-forth blame game with no end in sight.

Remember: the more he feels angry and defensive, the easier it is for him to feel that he's absolutely right about you—you are to blame. After all, look how difficult you're being! The proof is right before his eyes—at least that's how he'll see it.

Your angry or defensive behavior will only reinforce what he's trying to tell himself about you.

This may seem like a no-win situation, but it isn't. There is a middle ground between accepting blame for everything and just getting mad and throwing it back at him. And that middle ground is where I want you to stand if you find yourself in this situation.

There, in that middle ground, you aren't going to *react* to anything – you aren't going to break down or strike out. Rather you're going to *respond* to what is happening and the things that your husband is saying to you.

If you feel that your husband is trying to blame any and all marriage problems on you, if you feel that he's trying to pin his unhappiness or lack of fulfillment in life on you, I want you to slow down and, instead of reacting on impulse, I want you respond with a simple coin approach.

On one side of the coin, I want you to acknowledge the ways that he might be right. Nobody's perfect and there may be some truth in what he's saying.

Accept that and acknowledge it. This doesn't weaken your position, it strengthens it. It shows him that you're willing to look at your part. It knocks the wind out of his sails. He can't get too mad at you, since you're acknowledging that he's right about some of it…so there's no resistance he can fight against there.

Now, it's true that he might exploit this and run with it, but you have no control over that. You can only control what *you* do and don't do.

As you'll see again and again when it comes to dealing with a husband in the throes of a so-called midlife crisis, it often comes down to choosing the least bad option in terms of how to respond to him.

Regardless, this "accept and acknowledge" approach is the right thing to do in most cases.

If your husband is feeling unheard or unappreciated, you do want to acknowledge that. If he's feeling that past problems have not been fully laid to rest, acknowledge that. If he is still upset about past hurts or poor behavior on your part, acknowledge that—this could be anything from overspending or having a child-centered marriage to an affair or displaying chronic negativity.

Even if this approach doesn't work right away, he will remember your willingness to accept your role in things, and that may make him more likely to return at some point in the future to talk about the marriage.

So that's one side of the coin. Acknowledging his legitimate complaints about you or the marriage, regardless of how hard it might be do that. You'd want him to do that for you, right? So you do it first. Lead the way.

On the other side of the coin, I want you to shrug off the blame or accusations that you believe are untrue or unfair. I don't want you to be passive, but I do want you send the message that you don't agree and you're not going to listen to it. You don't want this to become a habit in the marriage.

Let's see this in action. Let's say a husband, we'll call him Jim, says to his wife: *"The reason we still have a heavy mortgage at our age is because of your spending. I get so angry when I think about what I could be doing at this point in my life if we weren't in such debt."*

Here's a possible response from his wife:

"There's a lot of truth in what you're saying, Jim. I've been very irresponsible and short-sighted at times when it comes to money. I know that's caused you anxiety and I can understand your resentment, especially as you see our friends already retired and living it up.

"But I also think that there were many times over the years that we as a couple could have sat down to budget. We always talked about it and we had the best of intentions, but it never happened. I think that contributed to where we are, too. And I think if we put our heads together now with regard to our finances, we could really turn this around."

Now, let's unpack this a bit.

By responding in this way, the wife did a few good things. On one side of the coin, she acknowledged her husband's feelings and the impact the problem had on him. Let me repeat that because it's important: she acknowledged her husband's feelings and the impact the problem had on him. That makes him feel heard, understood and respected.

On the other side of the coin, she refused to accept all the blame. And—very importantly—she did this in a low-conflict way. She didn't say, *"Well, you're to blame, too! How much money did you waste over the years on boats and golf memberships?"* Instead of saying that, instead of pointing the finger at him—something that would only make him react in a defensive way—she said something very powerful. She said, *"we as a couple."*

And then she aimed and refocused. She talked about the future and she expressed optimism that they could work together, as a couple, for a better future.

Will this response work? I don't know. Some men who are having a midlife crisis are determined to see the negative in everything. Some are determined to blame their wife or find fault with the marriage so they can justify their behavior.

In that case, it won't matter how well you respond. They have their agenda and they're sticking to it. It has nothing to do with good communication or logic. It's about what they want.

Nonetheless, this kind of response is better than those other reactions—accepting blame for everything or getting mad. This kind of response prevents that really troubling dynamic from entrenching itself in your marriage: that is, the dynamic where your husband blames you for everything and starts to see you as the bad guy, and where you inadvertently allow that to happen by playing along.

So think like a coin. On one side, it's about acknowledging his feelings, opinions, needs and admitting your own shortcomings and role in things. On the other side, it's about refusing to accept all the blame. Instead of just blaming him as a knee-jerk reaction, you can make it about the two of you. "We as a couple" weren't good with our money. "We as a couple" didn't always prioritize our intimacy. "We as a couple" never really learned to communicate well. That kind of thing.

And if on top of that you can aim and refocus, even better. Try to look toward a positive future, and making changes that will make life happier and more fulfilling for both of you.

Staying Connected:
Ten Crucial Tips to Keep Him Talking to You

Here in part one of the book, we're assuming that your husband's midlife crisis comes from an authentic or mostly authentic place.

He really is looking back on his life and wishing he'd done some things differently. He may be having some fear about aging and he may be feeling that life has gotten a bit stale. That's fair enough.

You may feel the same way. It's almost good if you do. That way, you can show empathy and make this a life transition for both of you, instead of a crisis for him alone.

Back when I was talking about the aim and refocus approach, I mentioned how useful it was to try to find common ground with your husband. In fact, whenever I'm trying to help an unhappy couple reconnect or move past a problem, one of the first things I do is look for that common ground.

That's because a couple on the verge of moving in different directions needs to feel a sense of sameness, that they're in it together, and that they have a shared identity, a shared past and a future together.

They need to realize that they're feeling or hoping for the same things, and that they have the same reasons for being unhappy, even if they're both experiencing that in their own way. So do that. Try to stay connected by finding common ground.

After all, most loving and committed long-term couples do want the same things! Financial security. Acceptance. A sense of adventure, fulfillment and happiness in life. They want to feel heard, loved and supported. They want to improve themselves. They want to have fun in life. They don't want any regrets. They want a partner who makes life easier and who's a wonderful companion. So find those shared interests and talk about them.

To that end, I'm going to give you ten crucial communication tips to use whenever you talk to your husband, whether it's a pleasant conversation about shared interests or whether you're discussing something more emotional and serious.

Too often, emotional couples find that conversations quickly deteriorate into arguments. That, or they just go nowhere. And that can make an already unhappy husband step further away. He may find it so unpleasant or pointless to talk to you that he just stops talking and starts walking…away.

So read through the following tips. These are the kinds of things that can literally make or break a conversation. Use them and keep him talking to you!

1. The first communication tip to keep in mind is as simple as it is essential. And that's impeccable timing. Wives often underestimate the importance of perfect timing, but timing can be all-important.

If your husband has just walked through the door after a long day at work, it probably isn't a good idea to rush up to him and say, "Let's talk, now!" The same thing goes for late-night conversations. People are often exhausted at the end of the day and just want to relax. Similarly, don't wake him up in the middle of the night to talk. If you need to talk before dawn, call an understanding friend. Put some thought into timing. When does your husband tend to be the most positive or open-minded? In the morning? Or maybe he is a night owl and evening is actually a good time. You know him best.

Scheduling a conversation can help, too. You can prepare mentally and limit distractions. Pick a time when your children or friends won't interrupt, and neither of you are waiting on some important call or email from work—you don't want to be checking your phone every five minutes during the conversation.

Spontaneous conversations can work, especially if you're both in a loving and open-minded mood. Use your own judgment, but don't let the clock run. Don't try to talk about everything at once or follow your husband around the house, insisting that he keep talking. Emotional conversations can't go on for too long. They're just too draining. Your husband will be more willing to talk to you if he knows the conversation won't be endless.

2. Different walls, or no walls at all. Arguments and long, destructive "talks" can be very predictable. Couples often have them at the same time, in the same room, and even using the same words. Shake this up by changing your environment so that it helps, not hinders, the conversation.

I've advised some wives to "get away from it all" with their husband and spend a night or two in a hotel so they can talk about their problems in a different environment.

Why have the same argument within the confines of your kitchen walls, when you can chat idly, romantically even, in a jet tub in a nice hotel room nibbling on some chocolate-covered strawberries? That can make a conversation feel and proceed much differently.

Or take a drive. Pack a lunch and listen to your favorite tunes as you drive to the lake. Evening drives can be particularly pleasant: fill a couple travel mugs with hot chocolate and drive into the country to look at the stars. Break out of your rut, out of your walls, and talk about things under the vast expanse of a beautiful starry sky. The sky's the limit for your marriage.

If your husband has a defensive streak and tends to get angry or argumentative, try an evening "walk and talk." Some husbands say they feel "interrogated" or "put on the spot" when their wife tries to talk to them. Walking together side by side can take the pressure off of a face-to-face communication and make it easier to open up. You can walk hand in hand, moving forward, literally and symbolically, as you have a relaxed heart-to-heart conversation.

3. Use humor. I've suggested to wives that they watch something funny or lighthearted before a serious conversation and to even take "time outs" during that conversation to find solace and perspective in laughter.

Similarly, don't be afraid to crack a joke or use humor as you talk. As long as you aren't laughing *at* him or in some way poking fun at what he's experiencing or saying, it's fine to keep the conversation lighter, especially if you're the type of couple that has a good sense of humor.

4. Remember the good. You might be hurt or angry with your husband right now, especially if he's re-writing your history. You might therefore find it all too easy to forget his better qualities, including the ways he has been good to you in the past.

As hard as it is, remind yourself—and him—of the ways he's helped you, or your family and friends, in the past. This can help you stay in the right frame of mind, instead of descending into criticism.

* * * * * * *

FROM DON'S DESK

As a man, #4 sticks out to me. Men absolutely love to hear their wives say thank you for the things we do. We love to know that you remember those things. It makes us feel good and useful. I would recommend that wives really focus on #4.

Talk about how he helped you finish a certain project, or what a good dad he is, or how he helped your parents with something, or how he helped your friend move...whatever, just make him realize that you "need" him.

And definitely, steer clear of criticism right now, even if you feel it's warranted (which it likely is). Men know when we've done something wrong or when we're doing something wrong—this is not the time to directly point it out, at least not if you want him to feel loving toward you.

* * * * * * *

5. Bite your tongue. As you and your husband talk through your problems, you will hear things you don't like. You may disagree with what he says at times, or you may feel very hurt by it. But remember this: As long as your husband is being open, honest and respectful of your feelings, as long as his goal is to reconnect with you and make you happy as well...as long as that's the frame of mine he's in, he's entitled to express his legitimate complaints.

Don't you *want* him to do that? You don't want him to stop talking. If he does, you'll have no idea what he's thinking or feeling, and it'll be easy for his thoughts to turn negative. So hear him out. Instead of punishing him for what he says, show gratitude for his honesty. By doing so, you set a tone that encourages understanding and cooperation.

6. Listen to yourself. Look at yourself. Make sure that your voice tone stays positive, pleasant and cooperative. A critical, sarcastic or snarky tone of voice will sabotage your efforts.

Also, look in the mirror. Now talk. Use the same tone of voice that you use with your husband—how do you look? That is, what is he seeing? Is your expression loving and open, or is it closed and critical? Stay loving and open, in both words and expression.

7. Have some humility. We live in a society that's becoming more and more narcissistic and intolerant. We're very good at expressing our own feelings and complaints, but we rise up in defensiveness or anger when someone else has the audacity to do the same! Show humility when you speak to your husband. Be sure to regularly self-check your attitude so that he gets the message you care about his happiness and what he has to say. Spend less time defending yourself or trying to prove how you're right and he's wrong, and spend more time trying to understand and empathize with his perspective. Admit to your flaws and mistakes. The more you do that, the more likely he is to do the same.

8. Get your outbursts and tears under control. This is an emotional time in your life. Many clients have told me that this is the most emotional experience they can remember having in their life. There's a lot on the line: Your past as a couple, your family, and your future. You're scared, angry, confused and sad. But letting those emotions get the better of you, and letting them erupt so that they're all your husband sees, isn't going to improve your situation.

As we go on, I'll be giving you some tips to help you control your emotions so that you can remain in control of your own life. Frankly, the more trying your husband's behavior becomes, the more you'll need to do that. But for now, just keep this in mind: Learn to control your emotions before they control you.

9. Don't interrupt—and mind your other manners, too! While you're busy monitoring your voice tone during conversation to ensure it stays positive, take care not to interrupt your husband any more than you absolutely must. Nothing makes a person feel less heard (and more annoyed!) during a conversation than being constantly or repeatedly interrupted.

You may occasionally need to interrupt him to ask a question or to clarify something he said. Just be sure that you aren't interrupting him to defend yourself, contradict him or offer unnecessary feedback. Your husband cannot and will not fully hear what you have to say, unless and until you have fully heard what he has to say! That's just part of human verbal communication.

In addition, be conscious of your body language and ensure it remains respectful. Don't roll your eyes, cross your arms or shake your head in angry disapproval. The goal is to keep the conversation going, not give him an excuse to say, *"Oh, what's the point? You're not even listening to me!"*

I also strongly advise that you steer clear of strong language, or excessive profanity when you're talking to him. Those things come across as very obnoxious and can easily make a conversation go south. Yes, we all have an inventory of curse words, but this isn't the time to use them. It just sets a harsh tone that isn't helpful.

10. Accept that this isn't an urgent situation (not really, anyway). Women are impatient creatures. When we want something done, we want it done right now. We want our husband to understand us "right now." We want our marriage problems to be over "right now," too.

I want your marriage problems to be over too, and as quickly as they can be. Every insight and idea I suggest in this book is geared toward managing this conflict and improving your marriage in the shortest time possible.

But it'll take more than one talk to get there. Things may start to improve, maybe even significantly, after a good heart to heart, but it's unlikely that one conversation is going to completely break through his midlife crisis attitude or behavior.

So try not to approach a conversation with that sense of urgency. Don't put that much pressure on it. If you do, you're only setting yourself up for disappointment and frustration. Instead, slow down, talk through it, get through it, day by day.

All right—moving on. Whenever you and your husband have a heavy or emotional conversation, try to keep these ten crucial communication tips in mind. If you want him to keep talking to you, he has to want and enjoy talking to you. That hinges on you.

How to Steer Him Away from a Midlife Crisis and Toward a Midlife Transition

Earlier in this part of the book, when I was running through some of the more common reasons why men experience a midlife crisis, I said that middle age is that time when life often (but certainly not always!) stops giving you new things. It's a time of transition. Our lifestyles are often in transition: the kids are gone or close to gone, we may be retired or close to retiring, or at least we're set in our careers.

Our bodies are in a state of transition, too. We're not falling apart by any means, but things are moving south and bedtime is a little earlier than it used to be. That's fair enough. Growing older, as they say, is certainly better than the alternative.

Our emotions and often our spirituality may be in a state of transition as well. We start to think about the meaning of our lives and our own mortality. We try to make sense of it all and find some comfort or reassurance.

Some people rediscover the religion of their youth. Others leave that religion and embrace another spiritual system, even one that might be dramatically different from their previous belief system. All of this is common behavior in middle age. And there's nothing wrong with it. It's a transition. It's all part of the journey.

With all these transitions in terms of our lifestyle and body and emotions and spirituality, it's no surprise that our marriage might go through a transition as well. In the worst of cases, this expresses itself as a midlife crisis where one spouse becomes self-focused, self-indulgent and turns away from their partner.

In the best of cases, a midlife crisis is more of a midlife transition where both partners make the journey together. They re-evaluate their lives and priorities and they make a plan, together, for the future. They transition into the next part of their individual lives while also transitioning into the next part of their shared life.

That's what you need to try to do. You need to try and steer your husband away from the way of thinking and behaving that we see with midlife crises, and toward the way of thinking and behaving that we see with more positive midlife transitions. If you put that kind of label on what he's experiencing, if you can help your husband see it in those terms, you can prevent his behavior from escalating to the point that it threatens the future of your marriage.

But how do you do this? How do you steer him away from the midlife crisis and toward the midlife transition? Well, one way is by taking the wheel. By taking the lead.

To do that, first think about the difference between a crisis period and a transition period. A crisis period is characterized by fear, by knee-jerk reactions and intense emotion. There's a sense of desperation and behavior can be extreme. Those are the same things we see in a midlife crisis.

By contrast, a transition period is more deliberate, reflective and considered. There's a sense of perspective and a long-term view of things. It's a more conscious process. It can be emotional, but the emotions tend to be positive: hope, gratitude, maybe some nostalgia combined with a sense of optimism and renewal.

You can take the wheel and steer your husband toward a midlife transition by, first and foremost, going there yourself. Lead the way.

Change the dialogue in your marriage so that you talk about your past with a sense of nostalgia. Put it into the context of your shared life in a larger sense. Talk about the future in a way that lets your husband know you're up for a change—you're open to new ideas and new ways of living.

Channel that fear that your husband might be feeling, and that might be fueling his midlife crisis, into a sense of freedom and adventure—here we are, with years of experiences behind us and years of experiences yet to have. Let's shake it up.

Let's bring our marriage into its next phase. Let's update it and our lifestyle. And let's do that with some class—together. Let's show them all how it's done.

Make no mistake: the dialogue and the attitude you bring into your marriage, the way you talk about what's happening, can very strongly influence how your husband feels and thinks about things. You can set the tone.

I remember speaking with a male client who was in his sixties. Their kids were grown and out of the house. One was in university and the other had just married. He wanted to travel to Peru, to Machu Picchu, and said that he and his wife had always talked about doing that.

Yet every time he would try to make plans to go to Peru, his wife would make plans to go see their kids. Their marriage had been a fairly child-centered one—something the husband did have some resentment about—but even now, when the kids were grown and gone, his wife still continued to largely live her life around her kids.

I suspect their adult kids weren't too thrilled about their mother's smothering either, but the husband was really fed up with it. He felt they were stuck in a rut and that life was too predictable and bland. He wanted to enjoy some child-free freedom with his wife so that they could rediscover each other and their romance.

But his wife just couldn't seem to break out of that headspace where her life revolved around her kids' lives. I also think that she had become something of a homebody. She had her ways of doing things and spending her time, and she didn't seem very motivated to break out of that. And so she missed an opportunity to share that midlife transition with her husband.

Instead, he started to steer toward a midlife crisis, growing evermore resentful of his wife and feeling that she was holding him back. I think in this case that was true to some extent.

Now, don't get me wrong—I am not saying this is what's happening in your situation. I'm not saying that you're holding your husband back. In fact, in the vast majority of midlife crisis situations that I see, that whole "you're holding me back" way of thinking is completely unjustified.

I mention this case only because I want you to do some serious self-assessment. Is it possible that you do need to break out of your comfort zone? Is it possible that you do need to shake things up and make a conscious decision to transition from your previous lifestyle into a new lifestyle?

That doesn't mean everything has to change, but it does mean that we need to take an honest look at our habits. We all need to do this. It's all too easy to fall into a rut in life, and it can be really comfortable in that rut. But if one spouse is too comfortable in that rut and the other one is trying to clamber their way out of it—well, you're going to have problems.

If you'll remember, fear isn't the only reason that a man might have a midlife crisis. Boredom is another reason. And being stuck in a rut is the quintessence of boredom. You do not want your husband to be bored by his life with you.

So lead the way. Be the one that clambers out of that rut, whatever that might mean in terms of your marriage and your lifestyle. Instead of waiting to see what your husband is going to do and then sort of reacting to that, flip the whole thing around so that he's following you, at least to some extent.

I remember speaking with this man's wife and doing my best to get her on that damn plane to Peru. She wanted to go, but she never quite got there.

Don't make the mistake that she did. Don't make excuses, don't put it off, don't let complacency kill your marriage. Look at your life and transition out of whatever rut you might be in. Take the wheel and steer away from this impending crisis.

How to Make Yourself an "Unleavable" Wife

Over my years in practice, I've spoken with many men who have been very honest about why they're losing interest in their wife and marriage. I've heard all kinds of reasons, but when it comes to a midlife crisis situation, I hear many of the same reasons repeated.

Make no mistake—a midlife man's wife is a reflection of how he sees himself. If she is always negative, if she has completely let herself go, if she has lost her zest for life, if her energy is low or she doesn't have any outside interests—that kind of banality, that kind of giving up, reflects back on him.

How he sees his wife is largely how he sees himself. You are, in many ways, his mirror.

As we move through this book, especially as we get to part three, you'll see that this often factors into why some midlife men end up having affairs, often with younger women, and why a small number of them actually leave their wives to be with their affair partner. She makes them feel younger, more energetic, more alive.

Many men think that a younger partner makes them look more youthful. It doesn't, of course. Seeing an older man with a younger woman only amplifies the man's age to most people. But a man who is in the throes of a midlife crisis isn't seeing the situation objectively. All he sees is a young and vibrant woman on his arm. And that must mean he's young and vibrant...right?

So what does this mean for you? Well, don't get me wrong—I'm *not* saying you should sign up for plastic surgery or kill yourself in the gym trying to turn back the clock. The *last* thing I want you to do is obsess about your age or feel negative about it. I talk a lot about having gratitude for life and every day we have, every year the universe sees fit to give us, is truly a gift. Our lives as women are bigger than just our marriages, and it's essential to have that kind of perspective.

What I *am* saying is that age is just a number. What I *am* saying is that it is in your best interests, and in the best interests of your marriage, to retain a youthful spirit. I've known thirty year olds who were old, and I've known eighty year olds who were still young. You've known people like that, too.

Take care of yourself physically, emotionally, mentally and spiritually. When you feel yourself veering into that rut—whether it's in terms of your lifestyle or your attitude or your habits—steer yourself out of it.

The best way to make yourself an unleavable wife is simply to live your best life and to live it, first and foremost, for **you**, not for him. Do what you can to be the kind of person that nobody would want to leave, whether that's a friend or your husband.

Middle age is a time of reflection. And like it or not, it is very common for a man in a midlife crisis to wonder whether he married the right woman. That's especially so if middle age hasn't brought the kind of success or fulfillment that people hope for. So do what you can to make that reflection as pleasant as possible.

Moving forward...I'm now going to run through a handful of traits that can make a woman "unleavable" in the eyes of a husband.

First, she makes him feel appreciated. A lot of men who have more serious midlife crises feel that they've spent years being unappreciated by their wife. That can make them look back and think "why did I bother?"

Be sure to express your appreciation for everything he's done over the years for you and your family. Be sure he knows that his work and sacrifices have meant something to you and that you appreciate him for it.

A midlife man and husband also wants to feel that his life has had meaning—and his wife can help him feel that way. If you have children, a great way to bring meaning to his life is to make him feel like the family patriarch. Like he has a legacy.

I don't know what your particular family structure or dynamics are like, but this sense of meaning is important to many men. If you can nourish it, that's great. If you have estrangements in your family or it's a blended type family with different dynamics, then help him find meaning in whatever way you think will resonate with him.

Let him know how much life with him has meant, and continues to mean, to you. How it brings meaning and security and joy to your life. You want him to feel invested in his life with you—that he has roots with you, and that those roots bring meaning to his life.

* * * * * * *

FROM DON'S DESK

King of his castle. Provider. Protector. Patriarch. These are the words that describe how a man wants to feel about himself. He is desperate for you, his wife, to see him this way. You have the power! Wield it wisely.

* * * * * * *

Another quality of an unleavable wife is that she's an interesting person. If he's stuck in traffic for four hours with her, they can pass the time enjoyably. They can talk and listen to music and tell each other stories. She knows stuff and she can still surprise him with that—there are still things he doesn't know about her. She just has a way of turning his head and piquing his interest.

She also has a generally positive outlook on life, and positive personality traits. She isn't overly defensive, she admits when she's wrong, apologizes sincerely and acknowledges how her shortcomings or mistakes have impacted her husband. She is physically affectionate and has a good sense of humor, and that makes her easy to live with…she speaks respectfully and with a pleasant voice tone. He doesn't have to walk on eggshells around her. She's also trustworthy and reliable – he knows that whatever happens in life, he can count on her to have his back.

After all, life can be unpredictable. There are constant ups and downs, joys and sorrows, good times and bad times. There are fears and disappointments—yet his wife stays pretty grounded.

Of course, she too has her good days and bad days, like him, but overall, she takes life in stride. She isn't the kind of person that's always on the verge of blowing up or melting down, or that's always anxious or neurotic. That behavior can be exhausting.

Very importantly, she wants him to feel good about himself. She wants him to enjoy his life. That means she doesn't micromanage or criticize just for the sake of criticizing. If he expresses a complaint or preference about something, she listens and takes his feelings into consideration. She makes her husband feel supported in his endeavors. She shows him affection and is generous with her praise.

She takes care of herself. Instead of trying to cling to youth—which is as futile as it is foolish—she accepts the years with grace and cares for herself, inside and out.

Yet of all these traits, all these qualities, there's one thing I tend to hear from men who consider their wives unleavable. It isn't complicated. They just say that she's someone they enjoy coming home to. They enjoy her company. So ask yourself: are you being the kind of wife that a husband wants to come home to? That he simply enjoys being around? Are you a good companion?

Now, I mention these particular traits for a good reason. Yes, they're the kind of traits displayed by people in long-term, happy marriages. But more than that, they're the exact *opposite* of the things that men tend to complain about when it comes to their wife's behavior.

Unhappy husbands, those husbands who have thought about leaving their wives, have told me that they feel unappreciated, and have felt that way for a long time.

They have told me that they feel there is no meaning to their life and that they find little meaning in their family life or marriage. They just don't feel invested in their marriages. They've told me that they find their wives uninteresting—boring, predictable.

They've told me that they have come to deeply resent their wife's lack of physical affection, her negativity, defensiveness or anger, and that they're sick of tiptoeing around her. They've said they're exhausted by her mood swings and that they feel micromanaged, controlled, criticized—nothing they do is ever good enough.

They've told me that she's lost her spark in life, and that they dread going home because she's such a downer. They're sick of looking at the back of her head as she ignores them, wasting hours on social media or staring at their phone or television screen.

This is hard stuff to hear. Believe me, I get that. And if your husband is acting like a self-focused jerk to you right now, it's really hard to stomach this, I know. But you need to know this, and I wouldn't be doing my job if I didn't talk about this in a very open way.

The fact is, many men who go through a midlife crisis become very reflective when they look back on their life and it is easy for them to grow deeply resentful toward their wife if they believe they've been treated poorly over the years. You need to know this, because if any of his resentments are justified, even a little bit, you need to address them. You need to acknowledge them. You need to talk to him about a more positive future.

Now, when it comes to these traits and behaviors, you as a wife could point to any of them and say *"Wait a minute—he's not perfect, either. He's the one being critical and self-focused. Why should I have to do all the work? Why is it all on me?"*

Well, it isn't all on you. But guess what? You're the one who is reading this. If he were reading a book like this, he'd get a similar treatment. Trust me, I have never pandered to men in my practice. But I've never coddled women, either, especially those who *may* need to hear some hard truths.

You might also point to these things and say *"Wait a minute, I've been doing those things all along. I'm a good wife. He's the problem!"* And the truth is, you might be completely right about that! This midlife crisis might be entirely on him—it happens, and it happens a lot. In fact, that's what we're going to be assuming in parts two and three as we look at midlife behavior that has escalated.

Yet in my experience, there's always something we can do better. It doesn't hurt to do some self-checking to make sure we're doing the best we can on our end. Frankly, we all become a bit complacent and fall into bad habits when we've been together a long time and sometimes we just need a friendly reminder to watch ourselves. Remember that my goal is to help you reconnect with your husband...to make him fall in love with you all over again, and to create a happier, more stable marriage for you moving forward. If you can look at your own attitude and behavior to make sure it's where it should be, that's only going to improve the chances of that happening.

Rediscover, Renew and Reinforce Your Emotional Intimacy

Because it's so important for your husband to feel more loving toward you as quickly as possible, I want to suggest something that I've found works well to help couples renew and reinforce their emotional intimacy—the sense of warmth and connection between them, the sense that they truly are partners in life and that they have a past, present and future together.

I want you to think back. Think back to when you and your husband first fell in love with each other. Chances are, you were curious about him and you had a genuine desire to know everything you could about him. You asked about where he went to school or where he lived as a kid or where his favorite vacation spots were. You wanted to see pictures of him as a kid. And chances are, he liked that. We all like to feel that someone is interested in us.

Yet as times goes on and marriages get a little crusty, we lose that warm curiosity about our husband. Which means that they stop feeling it from us. But that doesn't mean we can't reverse the process, which is what I want you to do here. I want you to rediscover your husband. I want him to feel like he's important to you and that his history is fascinating to you.

Right now, your husband is doing a lot of thinking about his past – as we've seen, he may be starting to re-write it and see it in a negative light. He may be feeling that his life has no meaning or that it's been a disappointment to him.

You can help change that. You can help turn the whole thing around so that he feels a sense of warm nostalgia, meaning and joy about his past. That will help him feel more satisfied and content both with his life and with his marriage.

To do this, you're going to exploit the fact that people love to talk about themselves. I don't mean in a self-absorbed way, I just mean that we love to feel that someone is interested in us and where we've come from or what we've done. It's human nature. We like to share our experiences and especially our memories. It gives us an opportunity to relive a time or revisit a place that held great meaning to us. We especially love to share our past memories with those who are important to us, like our spouse.

That's why I want you to take a little stroll down memory lane with your husband, but I want this to be a very visual stroll, one that really summons those warm feelings of nostalgia. You'll do this by using the street view feature of Google maps. Plan a nice evening for you and your husband. Make a nice meal, share a glass of wine or a cup of good coffee and then curl up on the couch. You'll need your laptop or tablet—your phone will do, but a bigger screen will have a bigger impact.

Using street view, zoom in on the streets your husband rode his bicycle on as a child. Walk up to the doors of his childhood home or school. Walk down the sidewalks he used to walk down with his parents. Visit the lake where he spent summer vacations. Visit the playgrounds where he used to play with his childhood friends. Sure lots of things will have changed, but with any luck, you'll be able to see the same field he played on in the summer and the same hill he tobogganed down in the winter. There's always a tree that's still standing or an old house that we remember thinking was haunted. Have fun with it.

Don't rush these journeys. Let your husband lose himself in the nostalgia and tell you about the people and places he hasn't thought about in decades. Ask him a lot of questions and encourage him to remember more and show you more.

This exercise can be a deeply moving one for couples. I've even had clients tell me that their husband broke down into tears while doing this. It created a much-needed moment of softness between them. Nostalgia has a way of doing that. It has a way of bringing our most powerful emotions right to the surface and really putting our lives into perspective. Sometimes when we're reminded of people we've lost along the way—childhood friends or family—it can make us cling a little more tightly to those we still have. That's what we want to happen here. We want your husband to realize that his life has been full, that he has had many experiences and journeys...and that the ones he's had with you are the best of all.

After you've spent some time on this visual journey into your husband's past—and remember, don't rush it—you can go on to revisit the places that have meaning to you and your husband as a couple. Visit the place where you first met or the beach where you went on honeymoon. Visit that cool art gallery in New York or the farmer's market on Salt Spring Island where you found that fantastic painting, the one that now hangs in your living room. Visit the first house you lived in together, or the hospital where your child was born or the waterpark where you used to take your kids.

You have an amazing inventory of experiences as a couple. This inventory binds you together and gives you a shared history. But it's a history you need to revisit on occasion so it doesn't become lost to time. It's a history you need to revisit on occasion, so that both of you are reminded just how amazing it really was.

This experience can strengthen the roots of a long-term couple's relationship and remind them that they love each other. It can make them rediscover and renew their life together, which can in turn reinforce their emotional intimacy. And if this can happen, it'll be much easier to avoid or downgrade your husband's midlife crisis.

Make Him Desire You in Bed Again: The Hottest Move Ever

When I talk about being an unleavable wife there's one thing I haven't brought up, and it's a biggie. I'm talking about sexual intimacy, the flip side of emotional intimacy.

Without a doubt, many midlife crises—especially the nasty ones that escalate—are fueled by sex. Sometimes a man has something to prove to himself as much as anyone else. This is especially true if he is starting to have, or worry about having, performance issues. That can be a deeply troubling and sobering thing to happen to a man. They are keenly aware of changes.

The Shut-Out Wife

If he's thinking less about sex than he used to, if he's having trouble getting aroused, if he's having trouble getting or maintaining an erection—these changes are definitely on his radar. They're undeniable signs of aging. And they can also cause a man to go through something of an identity crisis. Who am I if I'm not that same sexual being I was before? How does this change me and what does this mean for my life? Is that type of pleasure going to be a thing of the past for me? Is there anything I can do to get it back?

The impact of a declining sex drive or the appearance of performance problems is a complicated, personal thing. It manifests in different ways. If sex has been an issue in the marriage, especially if a lack of sex has been an issue in the marriage, some midlife men will grow more resentful of that.

I've heard men say, "I've been denied sex for years in this marriage. And now, with maybe only a few years left where I can really enjoy sex, I want to do that. I resent my wife for withholding or not being sexual enough. I don't care what happens, I'm going to enjoy it now while I can."

Again, my intention isn't to blame a wife or assume that a lack of sexual intimacy in the marriage was her fault. It's never that simple in a marriage and sex is complicated. Remember that my intention is to help you understand what your husband might be thinking and why, and what might be motivating his behavior. Because knowing that is to *your* benefit.

Yet regardless of whether there have been sexual problems in the marriage or not, that declining sex drive and those performance issues or concerns often factor into a man's midlife crisis. That's why I highly recommend you take steps to reignite the spark of sexual intimacy between the two of you.

Remember though, that sex isn't just about the mechanics. It's also about sensuality and mental arousal. It's about affection, eroticism and anticipation. It's about flirting and fun.

So do what you can to make your marriage a more sensual one, whether that means engaging in erotic massage or experimenting with Tantric sex. Make your bedroom a more sensual space with good linens and warm colors, candles and maybe some music. Redecorate your bedroom, going for a sexier aura. A change is as good as a rest, as they say.

At the same time, don't ignore those mechanics—challenge yourself to spice it up with new positions and some spontaneity. Move into the shower or the downstairs couch. Surprise him once in a while and show him you've still got it. Don't be shy—life isn't long enough to be shy!—and try some erotic aides like a vibrator or a blindfold or some restraints. Buy a sex book and learn some new moves or read erotica together. Sex is definitely a use it or lose it type of thing. So use it. Use it well.

Years back, I attended a conference with a number of colleagues, one of whom was very open about her love of men and of sex. She was very honest about the fact that her number was in the "very high" double digits. Anyway, a bunch of us women were in the lounge having a couple of glasses of wine and winding down from a seminar, when of course the conversation turned to men and relationships, as so often happens when women get together and the wine begins to flow.

As the night wore on and the conversation got a little more explicit, somebody asked this lady—our own Samantha Jones—this question: "Tell us, in your extensive and very personal experience, what is the hottest sex move there is? How do you really turn a man on?"

And then we all waited. This was so much more interesting than the seminar we'd sat through all day. She thought about it for a long time. Finally, she put down her wine glass, nodded her head in certainty and said, "The hottest sex move is enthusiasm."

Well. We were all very disappointed by that answer. We wanted details—a technique, or a twist or a turn that we hadn't heard of, but alas, enthusiasm was all we got.

Yet she spoke the truth. One of the best ways to reignite your sexual intimacy is to approach your sex life with renewed enthusiasm. With good emotional and physical energy. With a healthy attitude and a sincere desire to pleasure your husband, enjoy yourself, and strengthen your loving bond.

In fact, I think wives would be wise to show enthusiasm for their marriage and spouse in a larger sense, too, and that's what I've tried to convey here in part one of the book.

This doesn't mean shrieking with excitement when your husband walks through the door, but maybe it does mean getting up and meeting him at the door with a "welcome home" kiss and a flirtatious slap on the backside.

This doesn't mean blithely smiling or jumping for joy when you're trying to work through a marriage problem, but maybe it does mean trying to approach the issue with as much positive energy as is reasonable and possible under the circumstances.

A person who approaches life with an enthusiastic spirit, and who applies that positive energy to their relationship, sends a strong message—"This matters to me. I am interested in this." That's not a bad message to send. And here's the real bonus. This kind of enthusiasm is contagious. When a wife has it, she can spread it to her husband, and it can spread throughout their married life.

I remember speaking with a client whose husband was definitely starting down the trail of a midlife crisis. And it was escalating every day. He wanted to buy a restored Shelby, a really nice vintage car, since he used to have one when he was younger. Unfortunately, his wife was handling everything wrong, completely backwards.

Instead of showing enthusiasm for his interest and going along for the ride, (literally), she was just really negative and condescending about the whole thing. She had told him that he was just trying to recapture his lost youth and it was ridiculous.

But he wanted the car. He desperately wanted it. She told me about one evening when he opened up about it—a rare thing for this guy to do—and said, "I maybe have ten years in me to drive a sexy car like that."

Yet again, she handled it wrong. Instead of hearing that message and the plea for understanding and support underneath it, she told him he was silly to be thinking in those terms.

It was no shock to me that his midlife crisis behavior did escalate. He bought the car without her go-ahead. They continued to argue and grow apart, until he moved out and got his own apartment.

But things turned around after I spoke with her. Essentially, I gave her a dare. I dared her to book a road trip for her and her husband, in the new car. I dared her to be enthusiastic about this trip.

"Don't worry about anything, " I said. "Don't worry about the fact that he's moved out, don't worry what he's doing, don't worry that he might refuse to go, just plan it and move ahead as if it's happening. Lead the way."

So she did. She mapped out a road trip—it was down the Oregon coast as a matter of fact—and booked some really nice hotels along the whole route. And then she showed up at her husband's apartment with her bags packed and said "Let's go."

And they did. And it was the time of their lives. They drove a sexy car down the Oregon coast and—I'll say it bluntly—had hotel sex every evening.

My point is this: don't just be his bedmate, be his playmate. Inject some passion and enthusiasm into your marriage, both inside and outside of the bedroom.

Now, let me be clear. Here, I'm still talking about situations where a husband has not had a sexual affair with another woman. If that has happened, or if that is happening right now, I don't want you to be throwing yourself at him sexually. So hang on. We're going to be covering affair situations soon enough.

Right now, just do what you can to spice up your marriage in a sensual and sexual way, and to show your husband that you desire him. Show interest in him and enthusiasm for your life together. With any luck, he'll return the favor and you can avoid or downgrade his midlife crisis.

As with many topics in this book, I know this is a touchy one. Sex is a complicated issue and there may be all kinds of sexual issues going on in your marriage right now. There may be a long history of sexual issues or different sex drives or preferences. There may be a long history of resentment when it comes to sex, on either or both of your parts. So I understand that it may not be this simple for you, and this may be a sore spot. My goal here is not to oversimplify or to put all the pressure or responsibility on you.

My goal is simply to encourage you, if it's appropriate in your situation, to try and reignite that spark of sexual intimacy and enthusiasm between you and your husband, and to do that in a way that you're comfortable with. That's certainly a better approach than just letting that spark die out altogether.

How to Have a Better Life and Marriage Because of It

All marriages go through ups and downs. I'm not telling you anything you don't know here. You've probably had a gazillion ups and downs in your marriage, some bigger than others. If your husband is beginning to experience a midlife crisis, this definitely qualifies as a down period.

But here's the thing—even if he didn't go through a midlife crisis, even if that weren't an issue at all in your marriage, it's still very likely that your marriage might have gone through some other kind of down period at this time in your lives. Because that's what marriages do.

We start to take each other for granted. We become entrenched in our own negative habits and personality traits, those things that make us hard to live with and that drain the fun and friendship out of a long-term marriage.

We experience conflict and we stop trying as hard to move past it. We get complacent. We fall into ruts and we stop trying as hard to climb out of them and look for new adventures or experiences. We start to fall asleep at the wheel.

So in some ways, your husband's midlife crisis can serve as a wake-up call to both of you. It can be that red flag that waves at you and says, "Hey, time to start putting more effort into your marriage. Time to make a deliberate, conscious choice about what you want the rest of your marriage and life to be like!"

Earlier, I talked about turning this midlife crisis into a midlife transition. So do that. Talk to your husband about how important it is to stay young at heart. Talk to him about how you want to consciously and enthusiastically "update" your marriage so that it reflects where you are in life right now, and where you want to go.

Create a new identity as a couple. Accept the years and the changes with grace. Get curious about life and create new rituals in your marriage, ones that bring happiness, meaning and fun to this part of your life. If you can do this, not only do you stand a better chance of avoiding or downgrading your husband's midlife crisis, but your marriage can actually come out stronger than ever.

The *Real* Reason it Has to Be Good on Your End

Back in the days before cell phones, when there were only telephone land lines, a certain expression arose: "How are things on your end?" That is, how are things at your end of the telephone line? How are things in your world? Is everything okay? Any problems?

Here in part one of the book, I've kind of done that with you. I've asked you to look at things on your end and to make sure that everything is okay, and that there are no problems that you might inadvertently be contributing to.

Depending on the specifics of your situation, this might not have sat very well with you. You might be so hurt and angered by his self-focused, irrational, and perhaps even immature behavior that it's hard to hear someone ask you to look at your own behavior.

Nonetheless, I've seen many cases where a wife was able to take the lead and make changes that resulted in a marriage that was happier, more loving and more stable for her and her husband. She saw the door closing, and she was able to prevent that from happening before she found herself shut out of her husband's life.

But that doesn't always happen. There are many cases where a wife bends over backward to do things right, but her husband's self-focused behavior persists, escalates, toward a midlife episode. As it does, this husband will often do his very best to convince his wife, and himself, that she is part of the problem. And believe me, he can be very convincing.

That's the *real* reason it has to be good on your end. That's the real reason I've put so much emphasis on you here, and on encouraging you to be 100% certain that it *isn't about you*. Everything is good on your end. This problem is on his end.

This is an essential state for two main reasons.

First, the fewer legitimate complaints your husband can express about you, the better. If he wants to blame something on you, he'll have to make it up. And deep down, he knows that.

Second, it is only when you are certain that you have done everything possible on your end to improve matters, and that you have been loving and fair to his side of things, that will you be able to clearly see his behavior for what it is. Fair, but aware. That's your goal. It is only in that state of awareness that you will truly have enough certainty and confidence to expect—to insist—that he improve his behavior toward you.

As we head into the parts of this book that deal with a midlife man's increasing self-indulgence and even his infidelity, and as we trudge through the attitudes and behaviors he uses to shut you out of his life, you will need all the clarity, certainty, and self-confidence that you can muster.

You cannot be doubting or second-guessing yourself. You cannot be swayed by your husband's words or accusations or justifications. You *must* be certain and confident that you've done the best you can, that you have been fair to him, and that you've given him every opportunity, every open door, to improve your marriage.

Know yourself. Know your shortcomings and your strengths, and know how those have factored into your marriage. Know what is fair to him and to you. Once you know that, there is nothing he can say or do that can make you retreat into the confusion, uncertainty, anxiety and doubt that you have already been living with for too long.

Q&A's, Part One

The "Why's" of a Man's Midlife Crisis

What might my husband be feeling? What might his insecurities be?

What might his fears or worries be?

What might he be thinking or assuming about his life?

What might he be unhappy with in his life? Does he have any regrets or disappointments that may be factoring into this?

Does he feel bored or unfulfilled in some way?

Has there been any event in his / our life that might have contributed to this?

What might he be unhappy with in our relationship or with me?

But What About Your Midlife Crisis as a Woman?

What does "freedom" mean to you at this time in your life?

How will you foster and protect your own sense of freedom and well-being, despite your husband's behavior and what might be happening in your marriage?

How to Make It Better Instead of Worse

How can you support your husband's ideas or interests?

Brainstorm ways to surprise your husband by making a positive change in your marriage or lifestyle. Get creative and be courageous.

How can you help him manage or come to terms with any fears or worries?

How to Deal With His Declining Sex Drive or Performance

Brainstorm a few ways you can make your husband feel more sexually desired by you (by the way, this is extremely important even if you haven't noticed any performance issues with your husband):

When He Starts to Re-Write Your History as a Couple

Is your husband re-writing your history? How so?

Write down what NOT to do when your husband starts to re-write your history – that is, write down what doesn't work…because you must be clear about this.

Write down what TO do and/or say when your husband re-writes your history. You can use the statement presented in the book, or you can write your own statement.

When He Starts to Blame You For His Unhappiness

Write down what NOT to do when your husband starts to blame you for his unhappiness as he becomes increasingly self-focused—that is, write down what doesn't work…because you must be clear about this.

How will you respond when/if your husband blames you for his unhappiness? Think this through in advance so you can react positively. Write down your thoughts, keeping the **"coin"** approach in mind.

Replay! Think back to an interaction between you and your husband, one that you felt went poorly. Now replay that, incorporating what you've learned so far—might you have been able to handle yourself, and the situation, better or differently?

Staying Connected: Ten Crucial Tips to Keep Him Talking to You

After you read through these ten communication tips, jot down the ones that seem most helpful to you—these may be ones you've struggled with in the past but wish to improve upon.

What can you do to make sure your conversations remain loving, focused and productive? What can you do, proactively, to set your conversations up for success? As always, get creative.

How to Steer Him Away from a Midlife Crisis and Toward a Midlife Transition

Do some self-assessment: do you need to break out of your comfort zone? Do you need to shake things up and make a conscious decision to transition from your previous lifestyle into a new one?

Jot down a few notes: What has your husband always wanted to do or try? What are his interests, especially the ones he hasn't yet had the time to indulge? Is it possible that both of you have become too complacent? If so, how can you shake things up to make your marriage more interesting for both of you? Brainstorm away!

How to Make Yourself an "Unleavable" Wife

Jot down ways that you can do the following:

• Make your husband feel appreciated.

• Make him feel that his life has meaning. (e.g. if you have children, can you make him feel like the family patriarch?)

• Be an interesting person that can still surprise him (and yourself!).

- Have a generally positive personality and outlook on life.

- Have a youthful spirit and zest for life.

- Be a person that he enjoys coming home to.

Rediscover, Renew and Reinforce Your Emotional Intimacy

Jot down the places that you would like to "virtually" visit, places that have meaning to your husband or to both of you.

Make Him Desire You in Bed Again: The Hottest Move Ever

Brainstorm some ways you can make your marriage a more sensual /sexual one for both of you.

How can you show more enthusiasm for him, both inside and outside of the bedroom?

How to Have a Better Life and Marriage Because of It

Brainstorm some ways that you can create a new, updated identity as a couple. Be creative and courageous.

The *Real* Reason it Has to Be Good on Your End

Does your husband have any legitimate complaints about you or the marriage? If so, have you addressed those?

Do you feel confident that you've done everything possible "on your end" to improve matters?

As you move onto parts two and three of this book, do you feel that you have the clarity and certainty to face his attitude and behavior with confidence? How will you keep yourself in that state of being?

Part Two:

When His Midlife Episode Escalates

A Question of Degrees

Here in part two of this book, we'll be looking at what to do when a husband's midlife episode has escalated and is becoming more destructive to the life you share. The question of whether and when a man's midlife crisis has escalated from an impending or minor one to a more entrenched and destructive one, is a question of degrees, really.

Barring affairs, which we'll get to in part three, it's largely a matter of his increasingly self-focused view of life and his increasingly self-indulgent behavior. His words and actions will also become self-serving.

On top of that, your confusion and sadness and sense of desperation may also increase, making it more difficult for you to really see, with clarity, what's happening and why. That's why, in the following section, I'm going to give you something of a "big picture" view of things.

After that, we'll move on to how to manage these behaviors and this situation, because there are better and worse ways to do that. I'll present to you those insights and strategies that, in my practice and for my clients—women like you—have tended to be the most successful.

Fortunately, I've also had the benefit of working with many men who went through a midlife episode, but who decided, in the end that they wanted to save their marriage and stay with their wife.

These men have been brutally honest with me about why they said the things they said and why they did the things they did. That has given me a level of real-world insight into their mentality and actions.

And that's the insight you are going to benefit from here. I'm going to help you de-code what he's saying and doing, so that you can stop guessing and worrying and crying and begging and persuading and so on, and you can instead start responding in the ways that are most likely to stabilize and strengthen your marriage.

The Big Picture

I've said earlier that a man's so-called midlife crisis or midlife episode often has a fairly predictable pattern to it. Many follow a very similar script. At this time, I want to walk you through a midlife crisis scenario, start to finish. In my experience, there are six general phases to a midlife crisis—it plays out in six parts, which I'll summarize so you can see the big picture.

As you'll see, this depiction is of a fairly bad midlife crisis, complete with infidelity. No, your situation won't be identical, but you never know—this might just help you see what is coming up, or might come up. Preparedness is key. At the very least, it'll help you realize that you're not crazy and you're not alone. Many women have been where you are (and have got through it, I promise!).

Keep in mind, however, that this discussion is just about seeing the story unfold. Here, the wife is something of an unwitting player on the stage. She doesn't know her lines and she's probably spending most of her time trying to figure out what's happening around her. That's okay. As we move on, you can look forward to seeing this wife in the director's chair. I'll help you figure out how to change the story so you have more power. There may also be a lot going on behind the scenes in terms of the overall marriage, and we'll take that into account as well. For now, just read and absorb. We'll get to the rest in due course.

Part One of a midlife episode begins with a man experiencing an unsettling but undeniable awareness—the cold-hard realities and often the fears of middle age are setting in. He realizes that he's getting older. He's aware of his changing appearance and energy level. He may be facing performance issues or he may be worrying about that happening. He may be going through life changes like the kids leaving home or his own retirement. The reality of his financial or lifestyle status may set in—he may not have as much money or success as he'd always hoped to have at this point, or he may not have accomplished everything he had hoped to accomplish.

As these realities set in, he begins to withdraw from you, his wife, and he may become reflective and quiet as he retreats into his thoughts. No matter how much you ask him what's wrong or what you can do to make things better, he just seems to pull further away.

Part Two. Here, a man may begin to think a lot about, and even begin to resent, the responsibilities he's had or the sacrifices he's made during the marriage. He may overemphasize them or believe he's made more of them than his wife. He turns more inward and becomes more self-centered. This is where his wife may start to see him re-write the history of their marriage, and always in negative terms. He may start to blame her for his own lack of happiness, fulfillment or success. If they've had problems in the past, even the distant past, he may dig those up again and blame his wife for them.

Now, these two parts—where reality is kicking in and resentment is blowing in—is where we see the kind of behavior that I talked about in part one of this book, particularly re-writing your history and blaming you for everything. I gave you some great strategies to help you cope with those things, and to prevent the situation from escalating.

Yet quite often, too often, it doesn't matter what you do—the situation does keep escalating...

...to Part Three. This third phase is characterized by a man's attempts to reclaim youthfulness in some way. He may strive to feel like a younger man or to revisit a younger version of himself. In so doing, he may try to re-experience the energy of youth and a feeling of being attractive to women, especially younger women.

A common way that (some, not all) men do this is via a new health and fitness endeavor. Yet instead of just trying to eat better and get more active, his new fitness pursuits may become almost obsessive, as may his eating habits. He may try the latest health fads or whatever supplement or exotic food or health shake is all the rage. You may find strange leafy things in your fridge and mysterious juicing machines may appear on your kitchen counters.

He may join a new fitness club or take up a new hobby or activity. Whatever facility or activity he joins may have a lot of women in it—things like spin class or yoga, for example, are typically populated by younger women.

As this goes on, this man does start to look and feel better physically. He has more energy. After all, that's what happens when we get in better shape! Unfortunately, this may lead to a burst of egotism. He may become judgmental and critical of his wife, whether openly or not. He may see himself as being superior to her not just in terms of physical attractiveness, but also in terms of lifestyle habits and personality traits.

He may suggest, or even just privately think, that he is more enlightened or interesting or engaged with life. He may begin to feel that she is holding him back or that he can do better. If he is surrounding himself with other women, especially younger women, he may begin to think that he is better suited to one of them. After all, they're just like him. Youthful, energetic, exciting.

Moving on. Part Four is where he may redefine his life by inventing the "new him." To do this, he will build on the efforts and changes he's made in part three.

He may embrace a new kind of lifestyle in terms of hobbies or spirituality. He may rejoin the religion of his youth, or he may leave his religion in favor of another one. Again, this brings him into contact with new and exciting people. As a result, he may begin to think even more critically of his wife, again whether openly or privately. All the while, he is continuing to act in more self-centered and more self-indulgent ways.

Now, in earlier stages, such as the resentment stage, he may have tested the waters in terms of how much he could get away with—that is, how poorly he could speak to his wife.

If he learned then that he could control the situation, and that he could basically say whatever he wanted to her and get away with it, he'll definitely wield that power now.

He may start to re-write his marital history in even worse ways. He'll go from blaming his wife or being cool to her to criticizing her to the point of meanness. It's like he has no filter. If a nasty thought pops into his mind, he'll say it. He comes across as narcissistic and belligerent. He may have mood swings, so that his wife has to tiptoe around him to avoid setting him off, feeling more shut out of his life than ever. He may behave like this even if there was no trace whatsoever of this side of him earlier, even if he was a loving husband for decades before this.

Now because he may be looking and feeling better these days, he may over-estimate his own attractiveness to women. He is bolder around them. And it's right around now that he might begin or deepen a friendship with another woman. This is often, but not always, a younger woman. Quite often she is divorced or a single mother. If she is married, she may share stories of her unhappy marriage or cruel husband with him (whether it's true or not), and they will bond over this. Soon, they begin to text each other on a regular basis. They will share inside jokes, inspirational messages and they'll build each other up.

He loves the ego-boost of this friendship with a younger woman. Meanwhile, the younger woman loves the way this older man seems to venerate her—she doesn't get that from men her own age. And so they establish a close friendship, one that they both feel is special and unique.

They're amazed by how well they just "click" and the way they just "get" each other. Very quickly, their texting begins to take on a flirtatious quality and before you know it they're lost in the erotic thrill of it all. They're consumed by it—oh, if only they could be together!

As this is happening, the midlife man's wife becomes increasingly worried and hurt by her husband's secretive texting and his friendship with this other woman. However, whenever she expresses a concern, she is told that she is controlling or paranoid.

He may tell her that she doesn't want him to have any friends or that she's just feeling insecure or jealous because of the way he's living his life now. He may make all kinds of accusations and say all kinds of things; however, it's unlikely that any of it is loving or genuinely reassuring.

Now, at this point I'm going to pump the brakes and go down a different road for a few minutes. Because not all men behave with callousness or coldness during this "new him" phase.

Some take a softer, introspective or philosophical path. Some will say that they feel "lost" and that they need to "find themselves." Instead of saying mean or cruel things, this midlife man may say kind, even loving things.

He may tell his wife that she's an amazing woman and say how much he loves her for everything she's done for him and their family. He may act confused by it all. *"I love you, but I'm not in love with you. I need to find out who I am. I just don't know what I want. Please don't give up on me...but I need some space."*

Oh, how the mixed messages will fly!

If he is involved with another woman, he may say that his new friend "gets him" and supports him, and that their friendship is really helping him understand himself and figure himself out.

He may say that you and he don't seem to have anything in common—maybe you never did—and so he needs to pursue a friendship with this other person to see if he can find that connection there. He may pitch this as something that's good for both of you, and something that's in your best interest, too. I mean, you want him to be happy...right?

So regardless of whether his self-focus or self-centeredness manifests as mean, angry or aggressive behavior, or whether it manifests as lost, confused and introspective behavior, the result to his wife is pretty much the same. She's left in a constant state of anxiety, uncertainty and fear. She feels shut out of his life, his feelings, his thoughts, and his heart.

She may be feeling deeply hurt and threatened by his increasingly close friendship with this other woman. She may be feeling angry and betrayed and that the intimacy or privacy in her marriage is being violated. Yet whether he is mean and obnoxious or lost and confused, one thing is certain. He will continue with the friendship no matter what his wife says, no matter how much she tells him it hurts her, no matter how much pain she is in.

As part four drags on, things may continue to deteriorate. He may tell his wife that he wants to get his own apartment. He may say that he needs space, or that it would be good for the marriage if they had some distance or time apart. He needs to figure things out. Or maybe he will say that he can't bear to be around her right now, for any number of reasons. He's just growing in a different direction and he doesn't have anything in common with her anymore.

This may be motivated by a desire for space and independence. It may be motivated by a desire to escape the responsibilities and familiar, ho-hum obligations of daily domestic life, and instead live like a single man again, to come and go as he pleases. Remember, he is creating a new persona for himself here—and that requires some new digs.

In some cases, he will simply talk about moving out. It'll be an idea he fantasizes about, or perhaps a way to keep his wife on her best behavior. In other cases, he'll really do it. He'll find his own place and he'll go. If his wife cries or begs him to stay, he may react in a few ways. He may be completely and utterly apathetic. He may be totally indifferent. Or, he may be angry and insulting.

Or, again, he may take that softer approach. He may spin it like the separation is good for the marriage. It might help both of them find themselves…so he's doing it for his wife's benefit, too. He might say that it isn't fair to her for him to stay in the home when he just isn't feeling like he belongs there anymore. So according to him, he isn't disrespecting her by moving out, he's actually respecting her.

Now, if he begins or has begun a relationship with another woman, especially a younger woman, he will become more distant than ever. And more than likely, he will lean toward cold, mean behavior instead of the lost or confused angle. If he's with a younger woman, he's feeling a rush of excitement and elation. It's a massive ego-boost and that makes it easy for him to redefine himself. He has a new life. And part of embracing this new life is erasing his old life.

And as if all of this isn't baffling enough, he may show a total lack of remorse or empathy for his wife as he does this. It's as if the ten or twenty or thirty or forty years of his previous life, your shared life, your family life, never existed to him. He may pull something of a disappearing act.

Or, again, he may choose a different strategy. He may waffle between the two women in his life—his wife and his girlfriend—setting up a sort of love triangle. Of course, he's at the top of his love triangle. He may try to have the best of both worlds, perhaps coming home for a good meal now and then or to have sex with his wife, but then once he's had his fill, it's back to his new place and his girlfriend.

He may send his wife all kinds of mixed messages. One day he is loving and she feels hopeful that he will come back. The day next, he is confused or angry again, and she is devastated. Basically, he keeps opening that door a crack and then closing it again, keeping her confused—has he shut her out or not?

This part, part four, when he is living as the "new him," will undoubtedly be an excruciating one for his wife, especially if he's having an affair. How to compete with the fantasy of this new woman?

Yet even in the absence of an affair, this is still going to be the most difficult time. She will still have to compete with the new him and his new life. She will still go through those ups and downs of hope and disappointment, relief and despair, of feeling connected one day and shut out the next.

While he continues along his path of self-discovery and reinvention, his shut-out wife feels powerless. She may start to question her own attractiveness or desirability or worth. She may panic. Will he ever come back? What is my life without him? Who am I without him?

As the midlife man embraces his new identity, he shatters his wife's identity.

She is left to pick up the pieces of decades of her life, wondering if and how she can put them back together. She is at the lowest point in her entire adult life, and yet her husband may seem to be having the time of his life.

Eventually—and it may take months or years to happen—this midlife crisis will transition into Part Five. This is when the excitement of his new life, again whether he's had an affair or not, begins to level out. The fantasy of the affair partner or the "new him" begins to fall apart, and reality returns. It always, always does. After all, a person can only stay in that heightened, high-maintenance state for so long.

Here, he reflects upon the changes and decisions he's made in his life over the past months or even years. He also begins to consider what choices are in his best interests moving forward. Should he continue on with the new life he's created for himself? Is that even possible? Does he have the energy or wherewithal to do that? Is he starting to miss his old life and those in it?

If he is having an affair, should he stay with this person? Or are they too risky, too undesirable, now that the fantasy has worn off. Should he apologize to his wife and try to make amends so that he can return to his previous life?

He will weigh his options and think about each outcome. He will review his actions, and decide how to resolve the situation.

The way he chooses to resolve it, the way he chooses to end this episode and wrap-up this show, depends on who he is as a person, as well as his current circumstances.

He may choose to continue on with his new life without looking back. He may file for divorce and choose a new life with another person. He may continue to treat his former wife with disdain and to forgo any kind of relationship with his children. He may simply close the door to his past life as if it never happened and shut out everyone and everything permanently.

He may choose this resolution for a couple of reasons. It may be that his behavior and character is shaped by a larger personality disorder. That is, he may simply be a damaged or incomplete human being.

It is also possible that he does have regret or remorse for his actions; however, his pride may prevent him from admitting his mistakes and from asking his wife's forgiveness. He may not be up for the work of repairing the damage he's done, or he may not have the humility to do so.

On the other hand, he may choose to return to his previous life. This may or may not be a sincere desire. If, for example, his girlfriend has left him or he fears he will lose too much money in a divorce, he may try to reconcile with his wife; however, he will do this begrudgingly, as a sort of last resort or a way to avoid financial troubles. For those reasons, his apologies and recommitment to the marriage will be half-hearted at best. He may also carry anger and resentment back into the marriage. Because things didn't play out the way he had intended, he may continue to treat his wife quite poorly. He may be back, but he doesn't really want to be there. And it's obvious to both of them. In fact, sooner or later his whole midlife crisis is going to play out again, from acts one through six.

And finally, it may be that he feels remorse and even shame for his actions, and that he truly does wish to reconcile with his wife.

He may sincerely apologize and acknowledge the heartache and loss of dignity he has caused his wife. He may show true insight into his actions or at least strive to find that insight. He will show her all the patience and love she needs, and he will do everything she asks of him so that they can heal and move forward as a couple.

The Shut-Out Wife

Clearly, this last scenario is the happy ending his wife has been hoping for. This ending does happen – and it's definitely the ending this book is designed to accomplish. No guarantees of course, but that's the goal.

This brings us to Part Six. And this part is all about his *wife*. You can think of it as the after-credits scene. How she chooses to conduct herself after all of this remains to be seen.

Will she look back at his behavior, and hers, and feel that she was able to maintain her dignity through it all? Or will she look back and regret how she handled herself?

This too will factor into whether or not a marriage can move forward in a positive, mature way once the high drama of the midlife episode settles and life returns to relative normal. A wife has to be certain that her husband won't put her through this again—and that has as much to do with her behavior as his (more on this soon).

All right, that concludes my six-part drama called the midlife episode. Although I have found these phases to be fairly distinct in practice, categorizing them like this is artificial. The lines between phases may be clear or blurred in your situation, and your husband may or may not display all of these attitudes or behaviors.

Not all men who have a midlife crisis will follow this script. Nonetheless, this book is about seeing the big picture and being prepared for anything. It's about having the insight and strategies to deal with whatever your husband says or does.

Which leads me to an all-important point. If your husband does wish to reconcile after shutting you out, that must happen according to your terms, not just his. It is essential that you have handled yourself in a fair, dignified, and self-confident manner throughout his midlife crisis episode, so that he will treat you with fairness and dignity moving forward.

He cannot return to you begrudgingly. He cannot return because he had no better option! He must return eagerly, with love, humility and respect in his heart. The only way that can happen is if he knows he has no other option—because you won't give him one.

No matter how much you love him, no matter how many years you have invested in the marriage, no matter how afraid you are of being alone, you will not tolerate being treated poorly or run the risk of going through the whole ordeal again in a year or two.

And that, really, is why you need to start doing the right things, right now, no matter where you or he is in the process. It doesn't matter if you haven't handled things in the smartest or most graceful way so far. No one can blame you. But moving forward, it's time to turn this around so you are in control of you.

When It's Totally Out of the Blue: The One-Part Midlife Episode

Now, before I move on and we start to stock that arsenal of practical strategies you need to win this battle for your marriage, I want to mention one other scenario—this is the midlife episode that seems to come out of nowhere.

I've had many clients over the years who described a similar scenario, one where a husband's midlife crisis seemed to come out of the blue.

They describe a man who for many years was a loving husband and devoted family man. They'll often say that they had absolutely no indication, whatsoever, that he was in any way unhappy with the marriage.

He never expressed a complaint, never talked to his wife about something that was bothering him, never gave her the heads up that anything at all was wrong.

In fact, I've heard many women say that their husband was even *more* affectionate shortly before that out-of-the-blue moment— that moment when he flips the switch from being the man she knows to being a total stranger.

The Shut-Out Wife

I've heard women say, *"On Monday, he was sweeter and more loving than ever. He brought me flowers and he told me how much he loved me. He was so romantic, so attentive. On Tuesday, I came home to find his bags packed...he looked at me, without any emotion, and said 'It's over. I haven't been happy for a long time and I want a divorce.' And then he walked out the door."*

In cases like this, a wife is shell-shocked. It's like a bomb has gone off in her marriage and life. And as she's standing there, reeling from the impact and trying to regain her senses, trying to get her head around the reality of what is happening in this moment...while she's in this disoriented state, her husband merely walks out the door and doesn't look back.

Other women will say that their husband had been extra loving and kind for weeks...and then they'll come home to simply find a scribbled note that says, *"I've moved out. It's over."* There's no walking out the door, because when she comes home, he's already gone.

When these scenarios happen, women will say, *"I had no idea. I didn't see it coming. It was completely and totally out of character."*

This sudden change in behavior is so dramatic that many women actually wonder if their husband has had a stroke or is suffering from some kind of brain condition, like a tumor. That's how baffling and bizarre and unexpected this shift is.

Yet here's the thing. When we look behind the curtain of these one-part dramas, we usually see that it wasn't out of the blue at all. In fact, quite the opposite is often true.

A man's midlife episode often strikes during a time in his wife's life when she is quite busy. She may be trying to balance work or other obligations, as well as social or other family commitments. She has a lot going on. This can make it easy for her husband to—as sinister and dramatic as it sounds—kind of have a second or even secret life.

I have seen many of these scenarios play out the same way. As we learn more about the situation, we learn that the husband had been planning his departure for a long time.

In fact, in some situations, his excessive displays of romance or love—such as bringing flowers or even planning romantic getaways—can be a cover. They're designed to keep his wife in the dark, so that she doesn't suspect anything. They're designed to reassure her that all is well, so that he can take the steps he needs to take to ensure his departure doesn't negatively impact him.

For example, some women learn after the fact that their husband had been secretly re-arranging their finances or holdings to protect his interests. They learn after the fact that he had actually arranged to rent or purchase another property where he could live. And sometimes, they learn after the fact that he has been involved with another woman for a long time.

So as sudden as it seems, this "out of the blue" moment has actually been in the planning stages for months. There was nothing out of the blue about it.

When a woman is caught off guard like this, she's unprepared. She's unprepared mentally, emotionally, financially, socially. She doesn't know how to react in the moment or even the days to follow. She's stunned.

And guess what? That may be exactly why her husband chose to hit her out of the blue like this. He didn't want her to be prepared. It makes it a lot easier for him if he can just say "it's over," or even just leave a note that says it's over, and leave her reeling.

That way, he doesn't have to face her questions. He doesn't have to deal with her confusion or emotion. He can just detonate the bomb and walk away, leaving her sprawled on the ground trying to regain her senses. It's all about making it easy for him.

As we move on, I'll go into more specific detail about why he does this and how you should handle it. For now, however, I just want to reassure you that this happens all the time. If it's happened to you, if it does happen to you, it's not the end of the world.

In fact, many of these moves that a midlife man makes end up working in your best interests. It's strange, but sometimes an event that seems final or unfixable is fairly easy to spin around so that it works for you, instead of against you.

How to Deal With His Fitness / Appearance (or Other New) Obsession

When it comes to a man's midlife crisis, a newfound focus on fitness and/or on his appearance is often one of the first signs that usually presents itself.

In those cases where a man's midlife episode remains relatively minor and does not escalate, this can simply herald a common-sense lifestyle change. It's a smart idea to take better care of ourselves in middle age and beyond. Therefore, even though his new focus on health becomes a big part of his life, it's a part that his wife typically joins in—so it's a life transition and a lifestyle change that they embark on together. There is no major element of self-focus involved. He's happy to have her join in. And if they choose to cheat on the weekend with a piece of cheesecake or a tray of nachos, he's all in.

Things are often different when it comes to a midlife crisis that escalates, that is characterized by self-focus, and that leads to more serious marriage problems. In these cases, this focus on fitness becomes quite obsessive. And although it definitely has a lot to do with health and wanting to prolong one's life, it also takes on a fairly obvious—and sometimes obnoxious—element of vanity and self-righteousness.

I've heard from many women who describe a similar situation. Their husband goes from being a couch potato, or at least a fairly non-active person, to the world's greatest athlete in record time. He begins to eat better, although obsessively so. He is very aware of every single thing he is eating and may become angry or frustrated if he eats the wrong thing. He may start telling his wife what he will and won't eat, so that she can plan the meals he wants. Or he may simply stop eating meals with her and instead prepare his own.

Some husbands also begin to criticize their wife's food choices and fitness level, whether openly or just through those little looks and sighs that say, *"You're going to eat that?"* or *"You're just going to flop on the couch after dinner?"* When she pours a glass of wine to wind down after dinner, he might make a big show of putting on his running gear and heading outside to wear off whatever he just ate.

This kind of moralizing is very common when it comes to midlife men who jump into these kinds of life-changing fitness obsessions.

It's a less flattering aspect of human nature. When someone feels they've seen the light—whether that's with religion or health and fitness—they can sometimes feel quite superior to everyone else. They may regard other people are as less enlightened, or less informed, certainly less intelligent. They may send message that they're living life the right way, and you're living it the wrong way.

This can come across as sanctimonious and condescending. If it's the message you're getting, you need to shut it down, and fast. But be careful here. The last thing you want to do is meet someone else's obnoxious or condescending or belligerent behavior with your own obnoxious or condescending or belligerent behavior!

Instead, send a clear message of your own. I'm glad you're taking care of yourself, but I'm an adult, and I'm quite capable of taking care of myself, too. So in the words of Thumper the Rabbit, *"If you can't say something nice, don't say nothing at all."*

If your husband persists in criticizing your choices or offering you unsolicited advice, your best bet is to adopt a policy of shrug it off and walk away. If he's in the middle of a lecture about your choices, simply walk away.

Don't give him an audience. I don't know about you, but I don't tend to stick around and just let somebody rag on me. It isn't rude to walk away from this. It is rude to moralize in the first place.

Regardless, this may be a safer approach than what you might be tempted to do—which is to argue with him or point out his sanctimonious behavior to him. Both of those approaches are pointless and are almost guaranteed to worsen the feelings and dynamics between you.

But just one caveat here: remember in part one, I recommended that it's always a good idea to approach any conflict situation by self-checking your own behavior, first.

Is it possible that you could benefit from eating better or being more active? It's definitely true that our personal health and energy level does influence the health and energy level in our marriage. Healthy, active couples tend to get more out of life. They have more fun, they live longer, they enjoy better intimacy.

So self-check. If your husband wants to adopt a healthier lifestyle, there's no reason you can't take the initiative to plan meals that you know are in line with his goals. You don't have to do this all the time—maybe three nights a week you cook, and he is responsible for cooking on the other nights. I don't know the particulars of your situation or schedules. I'm simply encouraging you to work with him when you can, instead of setting up a dynamic where you are working against each other.

Nonetheless, in this part of the book, we are dealing with situations that have escalated, and with behaviors that are more extreme and self-focused. There are many cases where a wife has been exceptionally accommodating and tried to support her husband's newfound health kick, but his behavior is so inflexible, and his attitude so self-righteous, that problems are unavoidable.

If that's what you're dealing with, your best bet, and the lowest-conflict way to handle this, is to not give him an audience. To not listen to it. When he starts to be critical or condescending, when he offers unsolicited advice, shrug it off and walk away.

Whatever you do, do not get into an argument. He is already feeling negative and critical of you. The moment you start bickering, those negative and critical feelings only grow. The moment you start bickering or arguing, you only confirm what he's thinking of you—that you're difficult or frustrating.

The truth is, there are many things about a man's midlife behavior that are obnoxious. And there is no perfect way to deal with someone who is being obnoxious. There is no perfect way to respond, no perfect word to use. But there doesn't have to be. It's okay to do your best. That's all any of us can do.

Now, in addition to obsessive or overly strict food choices, a midlife man may also become very regimental in his exercise routine. Matters are made worse when he joins a gym or a fitness class. If he has to be at the gym every morning from 7:00 to 8:00, or if he has to be at his fitness class everything night from 7:00 to 8:00, it's only a matter of time until this strict schedule is going to conflict with other plans or with his wife's schedule or needs.

You might be nodding your head right now. I've had about a gazillion women complain to me about how their husband expected them to accommodate their exercise schedule regardless of what else was going on.

It's common for midlife men to become very protective of their exercise schedule. It doesn't matter what else comes up, they're going to that class no matter what. They are completely and totally inflexible. I've seen cases where a family member was suddenly admitted into hospital, but a midlife man insisted on finishing his workout before going to check up on them! His exercise routine becomes the absolute priority in his life, and he'll often expect it to be a priority in your life, too.

I suggest you handle an exercise obsession in the same way you handle a food obsession. First, self-check. Be sure that you're being reasonably accommodating. Join in or support him as much as you want. Buy him a cool water bottle and let him know that you're doing your best to plan social events around his workout schedule.

You don't need to do this all the time, of course, but if all else is equal, why not? It's the courteous thing to do. Make sure that you're not secretly resentful of the way he's getting in better shape, or that you're not secretly intimidated by it. If so, you're probably better off joining in than trying to undermine him.

But here's a heads-up about "joining in." When I say join in, I don't necessarily mean join the same activity or exercise class he's taking. Some men want their wives to do this. They enjoy going to the same class and they find it helps them both stay motivated and on track.

Yet not all men feel this way. Some just want their own space. That's fair enough. And unfortunately I've heard some midlife men accuse their wife of being clingy or of trying to check up on him if she shows interest in joining the same activity.

So by all means, go ahead and ask him if he would like you to join his activity or class, if you actually want to do that. Just make sure that you give him an out. Make sure he knows you won't be angry or hurt if he wants that time for himself.

If he would prefer to go it alone, you can still suggest other exercise activities the two of you can do together, preferably something you haven't tried before. Tennis, racquetball, mountain biking, skiing, snowshoeing, scuba diving, tai chi or karate. It doesn't matter.

By taking the initiative and by planning fun, active things to do together, you can motivate him to be more flexible, and to be less rigid about his exercise schedule. This can help loosen the grip of that obsessive behavior.

This approach also allows you to introduce an element of adventure and novelty into your marriage. It's fun to try new things. That's what keeps us young at heart. And if we can experience those things together, we can create a new identity as a couple, one that suits us in midlife and beyond.

Now, let's say you try this but it doesn't work. He just doesn't want to do anything with you or the activity just doesn't pan out the way you had hoped it would. If so, don't panic and don't give up. You still have another way to join in, and that's by taking up your own activity, preferably something quite different from his.

I had a client whose husband had joined some type of spin class and was very obsessive about that. He did not want his wife to attend with him—he felt he needed that time and space for himself—and he just wasn't interested in doing anything else. She'd made a couple suggestions, but he never showed any interest. So she dropped it, which, by the way, was the right thing to do. No point repeating yourself.

Anyway, we brainstormed about what to do and she ended up joining a women's kickboxing class—at sixty-four years old, by the way. And she loved it.

She loved the activity and the workouts, but she also loved the camaraderie and the new friendships she made. It was an unexpected perk. She had joined to show her husband that she could, but it ended up being one of the most empowering experiences of her life. Funny how that happens, hey?

Before she knew it, she was arranging their schedules around her kickboxing class and the socializing she had started to do with some of the other women in the class. To be honest, it sounded like they spent as much time drinking wine as kicking the bag, but hey—that's what life's all about!

Now of course, her husband noticed this. That's the thing about midlife men...when you take the focus off of them, they notice.

He started to ask her about her class and show interest in it. And so she began to show him a few things, but only when he asked. She invited him downstairs and showed him the proper way to kick the bag, and how he could basically cross-train so that he could strengthen his leg muscles even more.

Now in her case, this was the perfect approach. She may have taken the class to prove something, but she went in with an open mind and she ended up loving it. She found meaning in it for herself, and new friendships, too. That authenticity is what made her husband take notice. She didn't try to convince him that she loved it, she didn't offer unsolicited advice or suggestions. Rather, she just went about her business and eventually he is the one who started to ask questions. He was the one who asked for advice and tips.

And just a note here: that dynamic, that switch-around, is something I'm going to be coming back to often in this book. I want you to stop doing all the work and all the wondering. I want your husband to start doing his share, too. So we'll be revisiting this in other capacities. It's a useful strategy, and one we can use far beyond this issue of fitness.

In this case, my client was able to keep her power. In fact, she kind of shifted the power dynamics in her marriage, didn't she?

Instead of her chasing him, instead of trying to attach herself to him in some way or to grab onto the coat-tails of what he was doing, she did her own thing. And—as so often happens—he gravitated toward her. He started getting curious about her life and what she was doing.

Her new activity, this kickboxing thing, was interesting to him. And it offered something to him: a new way to train, a way to complement what he was doing. It also caught him a little off-guard. It wasn't an activity he thought his wife would ever do, so that was a surprise to him.

I was really happy with how this case turned out. I loved the fact that my client had empowered herself like this, and I loved the fact that her husband stepped up and noticed that about her.

He loosened up a lot in terms of his exercise obsession and the two of them actually fell into a really nice lifestyle. They each went to their respective activities a couple nights a week, and then they trained together one night a week in the basement: they'd take turns riding the bike and kicking the bag. Perfect resolution as far as I'm concerned, and more importantly, as far as my client was concerned.

Yet unfortunately, it's very possible that no matter what you do, no matter how accommodating or supportive you are, your husband's obsession with fitness will continue to escalate and to cause problems in your marriage.

It may continue to drive a wedge between the two of you, as you come to resent the sudden, dramatic change and the attitude and behavior that goes with it. The demands. The criticism. The sanctimoniousness. The growing displays of vanity. The self-importance and the expectation that everything revolves around his food restrictions or fitness schedule. The judgment as you feel he is comparing you to other women, more fit or active women.

That raises another issue. I've often found that many (certainly not all) midlife men who become preoccupied with fitness tend to join the kinds of fitness clubs that are populated largely by women. Many men in middle age are retired, semi-retired or at least at the point in their career where they have more flexibility. This means that they have the freedom to join classes that other men, younger men, wouldn't be able to join because they're at work. A typical scenario is a man who joins a mid-morning spin class or yoga class. This is a class that is typically filled with stay-at-home moms who are slipping away to the gym while the kids are at school.

In fact, I remember doing this myself back in the day, back when my son was in elementary school and I was working from home. The class had fifteen or twenty moms like me....and one middle-aged man. Most of us found his presence to be irritating. We were trying to get into shape and had deliberately chosen to attend a class that would be full of other women.

Yet a few of the women kind of treated him like a novelty and he would always spend about a half hour in the boot room after class talking to one in particular. They even started to go for coffee. I have no idea whether anything shady was going on, but considering my job, to be honest, I had to wonder.

My point is, you may find yourself in the agonizing position of wondering whether your husband may be comparing you to other or new women in his life. Is he actually doing this? Most men don't, but it depends on him and how his midlife episode is playing out. Midlife men who dip into egotism can certainly do this. But even then, it isn't about you—it's about him. It's about how he wants to see himself, and how he wants the world to see him.

In the next section, I'm going to talk about what to do if your husband's fitness frenzy comes with an inflated ego. And in part three of the book, I'm going to go into much greater depth about how midlife men tend to view and relate to other women, and what you can do about that. As you know, that's the part of the book that deals with inappropriate friendships as well as extra-marital affairs.

For now, the focus is on how to handle his fitness obsession—although to be honest, a lot of what you'll read in this section also applies to cases where he's taken on almost any kind of new obsession. I suggest you start by self-checking, and making sure that you're being supportive and joining in in whatever way works for you.

However, if you feel you've done everything that could reasonably be expected of you on your end, but he's still being too demanding or critical or sanctimonious, perhaps judging you or giving you unsolicited advice, then my previous advice stands: shrug it off and walk away.

You don't need to say a word. Why would you? What's it going to accomplish? There's just no point talking or getting into a dialogue when someone isn't really listening to what you have to say. Someone who thinks they've figure it all out isn't interested in what you have to say anyway.

There are times when arguing about something only makes us look weaker. It makes us look like we're desperate to defend ourselves. It sends the message that the other person's complaint or position is actually valid enough that we need to strongly oppose it. And so when we do oppose it, we actually do validate it, despite ourselves. And that's the opposite of what you want to do.

Shrugging it off or walking away does not mean you're admitting that he's right. Shrugging it off or walking away is about you sending a message—*"I've said my bit, and it's up to you whether you want to hear it or not. But this is pointless, and I'm not going to waste any more of my time arguing about it."*

Remember, you're not cowering and shrinking away. You can smile pleasantly (not snidely—there's no need for that) and shrug and walk away—he'll get the message. Sometimes body language is the best way to communicate certain ideas.

Again, I know this may feel like you are conceding or giving in or letting him get away with it. I get that. We all feel compelled to defend ourselves, to correct someone when they're doing something wrong or to explain to them why their behavior is disrespectful or hurtful. That's human nature. But here's the thing. Shrugging it off and walking away may be the only option that won't cause open conflict.

Now, all of this sounds good, doesn't it? Shrug it off and walk away. I hope so. These are realistic ways to respond, that's for sure. Frankly, they're all you're left with, because the alternatives are worse.

But a midlife man who is engaging in this behavior can be very challenging to deal with face to face. That's why I want you to stay grounded. Self-talk. Remind yourself that no matter what message he sends, an obsession is an obsession. It's a lack of balance. Focus on finding balance in your own life instead of trying to convince him that he has lost his balance, whether it's with fitness or something else altogether.

I don't want you to accept criticism or lectures from him, but neither do I want you to deliver criticism or lectures to him.

You're both adults. You both need to treat each other like adults. So stay balanced. Stay in control of your thoughts, your actions, and the way you respond to him.

When the "New Him" Comes with an Inflated Ego

There's an old saying: many women think they're less attractive than they actually are, and many men think they're more attractive than they actually are. This isn't always true, but when it is, maybe it's for a good reason. Maybe men, who tend to be the initiators in a relationship, need to feel confident enough to ask a woman out.

But when it comes to some men who are experiencing a midlife episode, especially one characterized by self-focus, it's very easy for that male ego to become over-inflated. And when it does, it can do some serious damage to a wife's self-esteem, and to the marriage itself.

I remember an extreme case years ago that involved a middle-aged couple that had been married for some twenty-five years. The husband was in the middle of full-out midlife crisis, one that had definitely escalated. He had whipped himself into great shape and the "new him" had gone to his head. He said that middle age and his new body had recharged his sexuality, and he was basically telling his wife, flat out, that she wasn't enough to satisfy his sexual needs or desires anymore.

Now, in this case, this particular gentleman had a reason for sending his wife this message. He wanted to have a threesome and he wanted his wife to be okay with that. She wasn't. Still, I remember him showing me some pictures on his phone—pictures of the women he'd contacted on some kind of hook-up site to ask if they wanted to have a threesome with him and his wife.

I remember him saying, *"I'm a very sexual man and this is the kind of sexual partner that I'm attracted to and feel most compatible with."*

I looked at the pictures. They were all of beautiful, twenty-something women. They were the type of women that any straight man, at any age, would be attracted to. That's fair enough. Women are attracted to young and healthy men, too. That wasn't the issue.

The issue was that he honestly thought he had a chance with them. I knew, being a woman myself, that these women would never be interested in having sex with this fifty-five year old man. Yes, he was in good shape, but he was not attractive by any means.

When I asked him if any of the women he'd invited to have a threesome had taken him up on his offer, he said *"No."* That didn't shock me.

Yet instead of humbly accepting their refusal for what it was—a personal rejection of him, based entirely on his age and appearance—he stated, outright, that he believed these women had turned him down because they weren't attracted to his wife.

Now, I will tell you—with absolute, 100% honesty—that this man's wife at fifty-five was a knockout. She was fit, she was stylish, she had beautiful hair and skin and a lovely face. She held herself with class and dignity.

To be honest, on a very personal level, I had to wonder what she was doing with this guy. Did they not have a mirror in their house? Or was she just so beaten down by him that she had no realistic or objective lens with which to see him and more importantly to see herself? That's something that happens way too often when a husband has a self-indulgent type of midlife crisis.

Of course, like you, I wanted to unleash on this guy. I wanted to say, *"Are you kidding me? Are you delusional? Your wife is gorgeous and you—well, you aren't! Do you have idea what these hot young women are thinking when they look at you? I'll tell you—they're thinking 'oh my god, I'd need therapy after that!'"*

But, of course, I couldn't say that. Of course, I had to get those knee-jerk thoughts and feelings under control so that I could deal with this couple and do the job they'd hired me to do—to help them work through this issue, without judgment, and see if their marriage could be saved.

And guess what? If your husband takes on this kind of egotistical attitude, that's what you have to do, too. If he says ridiculously egotistical things to you, if he struts around like he's a stud and acts like you're lucky to have him or that he could have any woman he wants—well, you have to do what I did.

You have to get control of yourself. You need to distinguish between what will help the situation, and what will make the situation worse.

Here's what will make it worse. Laughing at him. Challenging him or telling him he isn't nearly as good-looking or amazing or sexually potent as he thinks he is. Trying to reason with him or question his line of thinking. Calling him names or insulting his desirability or attractiveness. Ridiculing him.

If you say or do any of these things, you are going to trigger a defensive response in him—and probably a very indignant one, too—where he digs in his heels and tries to prove that he's right and you're wrong.

So we're back to it. We're back to shrugging it off and walking away, simply because there's no better option available to you, and it's better to do this than to engage in a pointless argument.

* * * * * * *

FROM DON'S DESK

When Debra advises you to "shrug it off and walk away," she's trying to prevent a pointless argument where he ends up feeling worse about you. But as a man, I think there's an even more important reason to shrug it off and walk away if your husband says absurd things, or things that are egotistical.

If you try to knock him down a peg or two by insulting his looks or manhood, or by telling him how pathetic he is trying to look and act like a twenty-year-old (even though this might be true), I guarantee those words and insults will hit home, and he'll remember them for a long time. He might remember them so well and for so long that they might actually become an obstacle to returning to you. As men, we often try to hide our insecurities and vulnerabilities from our wife. We need her to see us as strong and virile, and if she doesn't see us like that, our self-worth is annihilated.

Never underestimate the power you have over your husband, even if he's doing his best to convince you that he has all the power. He cares about what you think of him, even if he's doing his best to pretend that he doesn't care. It's just a front, believe me. So whatever you do, don't use name calling or character assassination or insult his manhood, attractiveness or virility.

If he is going to come back to you sooner or later, you have to let him save some face. He has to be confident that he can win your approval and respect again. If you call him a bunch of names, he may lose hope that can happen. So don't do it.

If you're already been doing it, stop immediately. Even better, apologize for it and say that wasn't what you meant. Despite how hurt you are, flatter him—or at least flatter the parts of him that you once loved and respected, or found desirable. That way, he will feel like he can come back, which is what you want.

It might be hard for you to hear if he's blowing his own horn a lot, but the male ego can be a shield. For men who have a lot of regrets or insecurities, it offers a way to create a really loud noise so that no one hears the whispers of pain, regret and insecurity underneath. You probably can't spare a lot of sympathy for this right now, but if and when he comes around, try to remember this. He needs you, he needs you to love him and admire him, and make his life worthwhile. I hope he gives you the chance to do that.

* * * * * * *

Thus far, I've mostly talked about inflated egos that pop up when a midlife man gets in better shape. He looks better, feels better, and it goes to his head so that he over-estimates his own physical attractiveness. But inflated egos aren't always or only associated with physical appearance.

I've had many wives tell me that their midlife husband suddenly seemed to believe that he was her intellectual superior. So he might say things like, "*I don't want to hurt you, but the truth is, we've never been intellectual equals. I've never really been intellectually challenged or stimulated by you.*"

They might do this in a spiritual way, too, perhaps telling their wife that she's not as enlightened as he is, or comparing her beliefs or faith to his own.

Another deep breath. You really need to see this inflated ego stuff for what it is. An attempt to sell you and everyone else a bill of goods—that he's better looking, smarter, more desirable, a better catch overall. He needs you and others to buy that, because if you don't buy it, he can't believe it.

As it is in advertising, so it is in midlife crises: the harder someone tries to sell you something, the more wary you should be about buying it.

In the end, your best and only realistic option may be to treat his over-inflated ego in the same way you treat an overzealous salesman. Shrug it off and walk away.

How to Handle His Self-Focus and Self-Indulgence

When a person's sense of self becomes inflated, they feel superior to others (or at least they're trying to convince themselves of that to feel better). And since they are superior to others, at least in their own minds, it is only reasonable that the world should revolve around them. They should be able to do what they want to do, and to indulge in the things they want to indulge in.

The Shut-Out Wife

The problem is, they usually expect other people to go along with all of this. They stop thinking that other people might have their own plans or preferences. They can become profoundly, even shockingly inconsiderate and self-important. That's even more so if they're an egotistical type to begin with, or if they have shades of narcissism.

I remember a client who was struggling with a midlife husband. It was their twentieth wedding anniversary and she had planned a romantic night for them at home, complete with an elaborate fondue and a couple of their favorite movies. Her husband knew that she had it planned. She'd reminded him about a thousand times and texted him, and he confirmed that, yes, he'd come home straight after his workout at the gym.

You know how this story ends, don't you? Class ended at 7:00, so his wife expected him home by 7:30. The cheese was melted, the bread and fruit were cut into cute little cubes, the wine was breathing. The fire was crackling and the movie was cued up...she just had to press the play button.

Seven-thirty came and went. Eight o'clock came and went. She texted him, but got reply. Eight-thirty came and went. She texted him again. *"Are you okay? Where are you?"* But there was no reply. Nine o'clock, 9:30...and at around 9:45, he comes home. Of course, the cheese and bread and fruit are all dried up, the wine bottle's empty and the fire's been out for an hour.

"Where were you?" She asks him. *"Didn't you remember our evening?"*

"Yes, I remembered," he said, *"but everybody was going out for drinks after class so I went."*

Of course, this descended into your typical argument where she accused her husband of being inconsiderate and callous and selfish. And do you know what he said? He told her that it was her fault because she was putting too many demands on his time. This illustrates my point about how futile these pointless arguments are!

This husband knew full well that he was being selfish and inconsiderate, but there was no way in the world he was going to admit to that or apologize, at least not in any kind of sincere way. Instead, he did what almost all men do when they're in the throes of a self-focused midlife episode that has escalated—they find a way to turn it all around and blame it on their wife.

As this couple's pointless argument continued, she tried to tell him how hurt she was. She said things like, *"You hurt my feelings,* "and *"Do you have any idea how insignificant this makes me feel?"*

Again, all pointless.

Her husband simply reiterated that he didn't intend to do that, and that he had no control over how she chose to react to things.

Then, to make matters worse, he accused her of having no life and of basing her entire life around him. He made it sound like he was this in-demand guy with a full social life, while she was this friendless woman who lived only for him.

So, two things to remember, here. The first is the usefulness of the simple shrug it off and walk away approach. In this case, it would have prevented a pointless argument.

Second, try to steer clear of telling your husband how you "feel." He's not listening and he doesn't care. If he cared (at least right now), he wouldn't do it in the first place!

So stop trying to garner sympathy or understanding or compassion from someone who just isn't willing to give it to you.

Avoid saying, *"You made me feel sad"* or *"You made me feel unimportant or unloved"* or things like that. Those sound weak. They reinforce the message that he has power over you and that he's in control of the situation, while you're just living in his wake.

If you really can't stop yourself from saying something or commenting on his behavior, keep it factual and use more confident language. *"That was very rude."* And then leave it at that. If he digs in and disagrees—you know what I'm going to say. Shrug it off and walk away.

You must be able to rely on your own assessment of the situation and of what kind of behavior is respectful and courteous. You must be able to keep some emotional distance from his behavior, and never take it personally.

His words and his actions, his self-focus and his self-importance, they aren't about you. They're about him, and what he's going through. He might think the world should revolve around him right now, but that doesn't mean you can't break orbit.

Why You Need to Respond, Not React: Don't Be His Opponent!

When a man's sense of self is inflated, when he is purely self-focused, he can say and do some pretty heartless things to his wife. The attitude and behaviors he exhibits during his midlife episode can create all kinds of feelings in her—sadness, worry, insecurity, betrayal, anxiety, anger, uncertainty.

Part of his behavior may stem from the thoughtless haze of what he's going through. He's caught up in himself. He doesn't have a filter, and he doesn't care to have one, at least not right now.

Another part of his behavior may be more consciously strategic and self-serving. He may be fully aware of what he's saying and doing, and he may have a reason for it all: he wants his wife to react in a certain way. He has an endgame.

A simple example of this is a man who blames his wife for all the problems in the marriage, perhaps claiming that she's always angry or negative.

Well, let me ask you—how would anyone react when someone makes this accusation? Well, they get angry of course! They react in a negative way.

So when his wife reacts exactly as he knew she would—angrily, negatively—he gets to point to her and say, *"See? There you go again. Angry and negative. Just like I said."*

This reaction allows him to justify and rationalize his self-indulgent behavior and the way he is mistreating or disrespecting her. If he can get her to react in a negative way, he can go along with his own fiction—that she's a negative person and he has every right to do what he's doing.

And for the record, this kind of strategy isn't restricted to men who are experiencing a so-called midlife crisis. We all know what it means to "push someone's buttons." Many people do this now and then, depending on who they're dealing with and what their endgame is.

The same holds true for many of the other behaviors, attitudes and manipulations you'll read about in this book. They certainly aren't exclusive to men as a gender, or men who are going through this. Many of them are typical of negative or manipulative human interactions in a more general sense. It's just that we see tend to see them cluster around midlife episodes, particularly those really self-focused and marriage-shattering ones.

In any event—and whether you're dealing with a difficult spouse or a difficult friend, child, sibling or colleague—it's very important that you learn to tell the difference between a reaction and a response.

That distinction is an important one and it's one that you're going to rely on as we move forward, and as you learn to deal with your husband's challenging and sometimes hurtful words and behaviors.

A reaction happens quickly, often without any thought. We react from a place of emotion. There's a time and place for that (like if a bear is chasing you), but I would argue that this isn't that time.

Reacting is kind of involuntary. When we react to a certain stimulus—say, something our spouse says or does—we don't exhibit conscious control over ourselves or the situation. The reaction just happens. Our buttons are pushed, and we immediately react. That's why we often say or do things that aren't in our best interests or that we regret later: *"Damn, I wish I wouldn't have said / done that."*

Plus, when we react to something, we often come across as out of control as we feel. That doesn't help us look or feel empowered in our relationship.

A response, on the other hand, is more measured. It's more thought out and conscious. It may have an emotional element to it—we're dealing with an emotional situation here—but a response isn't overwhelmed by emotion.

When we respond to a certain stimulus—something our spouse says or does—we have complete control over ourselves. Our buttons are pushed, but it's like there's an extra circuit that the impulse needs to go through, and that slows things down for an imperceptible beat of time as we process it. And yet that micro-moment of extra time is still long enough for us to respond better, and to say or do things that are more likely to be in our best interests. We're far more likely to look back on our response without regret: *"He really pushed my buttons, but I'm so glad I didn't react or say something stupid."*

And here's another major perk. We don't just feel more in control and conduct ourselves in a more controlled way, we also come across as a more in-control person to others. We come across as someone who is more empowered and aware, and thus harder to manipulate. That gives us an incredible amount of personal power. And if you're dealing with a spouse whose midlife crisis is escalating, you need all the personal power you can get.

If your husband's midlife episode is indeed escalating, he may want and need you to react in certain ways. When he pushes your buttons, he may want you to be angry or adversarial, or confused or insecure, or defensive or hurt. He may need you to erupt in rage, break down into tears, or say something awful to him.

Those reactions help him write his narrative. They help him justify and rationalize what he's doing and how he's feeling. They make it easy for his behavior and attitude to escalate even further.

A man in the throes of a midlife episode will often try to set things up between he and his wife like some kind of duel—he needs her to be his opponent in some ways. He needs her to be resisting him, clashing swords with him. When she doesn't do that, when she refuses to engage in this match and instead shrugs it off and walks away, she doesn't play his game. She doesn't react in the way he has set her up to react. Instead, she responds. And by responding, she remains in control of herself. She keeps her personal power.

That is something that every woman needs to do, but it's even more important if she is dealing with a husband who is exhibiting challenging or manipulative behavior during a midlife episode. Don't play the part of his unwitting opponent!

Remember, the more you can respond to his words and actions instead of merely reacting to them, the more your husband will realize that he cannot manipulate you. The more he will realize that you are someone who is in control of her own thoughts, emotions and behavior.

Now, how will he react to all of this? Hopefully, with respect. Hopefully, it will help prevent his behavior from escalating. But don't count on it. He may respond negatively.

Picture two people in a fencing match. The first person isn't playing fairly, so the second person drops their foil and won't pick it up. The first person desperately wants them to pick it up, and when they won't, they might become fairly worked up.

They might shout, insult, or say awful things. They might try to bully or intimidate the second person into picking up their foil. They might threaten to never play with that person again if they won't do it. They might stomp away in anger.

But in the end, it's obvious what's happening. They're losing control over the game, and they know it. And the worst thing the second person can do is fall for it and pick up the foil. If they do, they're right back where they started! They might be better off leaving the foil lying on the ground, shrugging the whole thing off, and walking away.

A quick note: Despite what is happening, you should be able to reasonably and respectfully assert yourself in your marriage. If you feel you cannot, if you're concerned about your husband's possible reactions or his or your extremes of emotion or behavior, then seek assistance from a mental health professional or other resource. Such cases go beyond the scope of this book. This applies not just to this section, but to everything you read herein.

When (and Why) He Sees You as the Problem

As I talked about back in part one, it's quite common for men who have a midlife crisis to blame their wife for their own unhappiness. I gave you some strategies there for handling that in a positive way before it escalates. Here, we're dealing with behavior that unfortunately has escalated.

Many husbands who have more serious midlife crises, ones where they treat their wives with disrespect, will try to pin all their problems or all the marriage problems on their wife. And as their midlife crisis escalates, so too do the accusations. For the midlife man, this has to happen. He has to be able to paint his wife as the bad guy. Because the worse she is, the easier it is for him to justify and excuse his own behavior.

Now, might you your husband have some legitimate resentment and complaints about the marriage? Absolutely! I'm sure he does. As I've encouraged you to do in part one and elsewhere, you do need to self-check to make sure you're addressing his legitimate complaints. Admit to those. Acknowledge them. Make him feel heard.

Nonetheless, some midlife men are determined to lay all the blame at their wife's feet. Which begs the question: what do you do when your husband sees you as the problem? I'll tell you what most women do. They argue. They defend themselves. And guess what? It doesn't work. He's ready for that.

The Shut-Out Wife

As I've already pointed out—and it's so important to remember!—as soon as you start arguing, you reinforce everything he thinks or is trying to think about you. You reinforce all the negative things he is telling himself about you. You reinforce the narrative he is spinning.

I want to share a quick story with you.

I was in a meeting many years ago when a female employee stood up and basically tore into a male colleague of hers. She was accusing him of this and that, in quite an insulting way, and it was pretty obvious that she was trying to pin a certain problem on him. I remember this man standing up, collecting his papers, and simply walking out the door as she continued to talk to the back of his head.

He left the room and she was left standing there, looking like something of a fool. His walking away, his refusal to engage her while she was being disrespectful, shone the spotlight on her unreasonable behavior.

To me, that man behaved in an incredibly self-confident and powerful way. He showed dignity and composure. I have no doubt that his blood was boiling and his mind was racing with the all the things he wanted to say in response, all the ways he wanted to correct her or defend himself or point out her faults. Instead, he sent a powerful message: This person's behavior is so unreasonable and disrespectful that I'm not going to listen it.

I received that message, loud and clear. So did everyone else in the room. So did the woman who was trying to pin the problem on him.

He showed her, through his body language, that he simply wouldn't listen to him while she spoke to him like that. Had she remained seated and spoken respectfully, had she come across as someone who was actually willing to listen to him and work with him to resolve the problem, I have no doubt he would have responded in kind.

And of course, the next time she had to face him in a meeting, she was far better behaved. She had to be. She knew he wouldn't just sit there and take it if she just let loose on him or tried to pin everything on him.

Now, just think for a moment about how things might have played out if he would have engaged with this woman—if he would have yelled back or tried to defend himself. There's a good chance he would've looked weaker, maybe even guilty.

Of course, he had to respond to what she was saying at some point—that was part of his job—but he didn't have to respond under those conditions. He knew it was pointless.

He knew she wasn't listening, and that she had her own agenda and wasn't about to share the floor with him. (And the by way, this is a good example of how both women and men can use many of these unflattering tactics in a way that serves their purpose!)

Now, all of this sounds good, doesn't it? Shrug it off and walk away. I hope so. This is a realistic way to respond, that's for sure. Sometimes that's all you're left with, because the alternatives are worse. Will your husband like this? Of course not. If he's trying to pin the problem on you, it may annoy him that you keep moving around so he can't do that.

It might make him mad. He might say that you don't care, or you never listen. He might say you're being rude or disrespectful by walking away. And when he says those things, you might feel compelled to defend yourself or explain yourself.

I urge you to think twice: again, there is no point getting into a dialogue with someone who isn't really listening to what you have to say. Just remember that shrugging it off and walking away does not mean that you don't care or that you're dismissing his legitimate complaints. It just means that you're not going to be someone's whipping girl. It just means that you're not going to engage in a pointless argument that will only make matters worse and reinforce the negative things he may be telling himself about you.

When you shrug it off and walk away, do it with respect for yourself, but also with respect for your husband, even if he's not showing you the same respect right now. Don't be contemptuous. Don't call him names or insult him (remember what Don said about this—your husband has to be able to save some face to return to you). You can send him the message that you don't agree, that you're not going to listen to it, but you can send this in a way that increases your empowerment and dignity instead of decreasing them.

When (and Why) He Acts Confused or Unsure About the Marriage: ("*I don't know what I want*" or "*I need space*")

When a woman is faced with her husband's serious, self-focused midlife crisis, she also goes into crisis mode. After all, she's suddenly living with a total stranger.

She's suddenly living with a man she used to feel connected to, whose life used to gel with hers—but now, she can't even have a meaningful conversation with him. Now, the things he does and the things he says are baffling, hurtful, confusing. It's like he's been abducted by aliens.

Earlier in this book, I talked about how some women are so shocked and upset by their husband's sudden change that they wonder if he's had a stroke or if he has a brain tumor. That's how dramatic the change can be.

When a woman goes through this, everything that is happening to her is so bizarre, so unbelievable that she might assume her situation is unique. That can make her feel quite isolated.

But she's not alone, and neither are you. I've had more women than I can remember describe the same scenarios to me, time and time again. The behaviors that men in a midlife crisis exhibit can be amazingly similar. Sometimes, they even say the same things, word for word. And a common thing they say is this: "*I don't know what I want." I'm confused.*"

Again, he might be confused. Life and aging can be confusing. But his wife is confused, too. And what do people do when they're confused? What do they do when they don't understand something?

Well, they ask questions! So a wife might ask, *"What are you confused about? What is wrong? What is making you unhappy? What do you mean that you don't know what you want? What have I done? What can I do? How can we fix this?"* And so on and so on.

Yet—and you may have already discovered this—he either cannot or will not answer those questions. Instead, he likely responds by saying he doesn't know, he can't explain it. He may even grow irritated by your constant barrage of questions.

It may be true that he doesn't know what he wants and he isn't entirely sure why he's unhappy. It may be true that he is confused. But in the end, it is disrespectful and unfair of him to pass his confusion onto you, particularly when it becomes chronic, begins to negatively affect your marriage and your well-being, and when he isn't taking appropriate steps to figure it out.

If he cannot or will not answer your questions as to why he's confused, I highly recommend that you stop asking him about it. Again, it is pointless. It's only going to make him feel more irritated toward you, while at the same time causing your frustration, anxiety, sadness and worry to skyrocket.

Also, I want to give you a heads up, here. Sometimes, a person will start saying "I don't know what I want" for very specific reasons.

First, that statement—I don't know!—is a powerful one. By that, I mean that the person saying it gets to have all the power. Why? Because he's the only one capable of answering that question. That upends the normal, healthy balance of power in a marriage and basically gives him more of it, while you're relegated to simply worrying and asking questions…questions that he cannot or will not answer. In fact, saying "I don't know what I want" is one of the primary ways a self-focused husband can shut out his wife.

Let's face it. His uncertainty and confusion is a scary thing. It feels like he has one foot out the door.

As a result, you have to tiptoe around him, existing on the outskirts of his life, making sure everything is just right in his world so that you won't push him over the threshold and he'll walk out for good.

But when you think about it, that sets up a pretty nice situation for him, doesn't it? It allows his self-importance to grow as your home life basically revolves around him and his needs.

To be sure, not all men do this in a conscious or deliberate way. But some do.

Second, that sentiment—I don't know what I want!—can be part of a larger strategy, one that indicates his midlife crisis may escalate even more very soon.

For example, if a man says *"I don't know if I'm attracted to you anymore"* or *"I don't know if I ever really felt passion for you"* or *"I don't know if we should've gotten married in the first place,"* well, when he says those things, he's basically giving himself an excuse to disrespect his own marriage. He may be setting things up so that, when he goes on act worse or move out of the home, he already has that justification in place. He can say, *"Well, what did you expect? You knew I wasn't happy."*

In some cases, a man in the throes of a midlife episode may say things like *"I don't know if I ever loved you"* as a way to more or less test the waters. That is, he may be seeing what he can get away with—he needs to know how far he can push his wife and still maintain the security of the marriage.

As their self-centered behavior escalates, some men—certainly not all, by any means, but *some*—start to think about what it would be like to be with another woman, or to get their own place and be free from the obligations and limitations of married life.

While some men will just do those things without warning, others will lead up to those big steps by sending their wife the message that their commitment to the marriage, and their love for her, aren't rock-solid.

So then when they hook up with another woman or move out of the house, there's already a rationalization in place for the behavior, and they can more or less defend it.

Now, when a midlife spouse acts confused about his own marriage, when he openly questions the passion or commitment he feels for his wife, he usually choose one of two approaches.

The first is to be mean. Men in the throes of a midlife crisis can say some incredibly hurtful things to their wife. They may be openly mean and just blurt out things like, "*I'm not attracted to you. I never was. I don't know if I can stay in a marriage where I don't feel passion for my wife.*"

The second approach is a little safer. They may wrap their confusion and uncertainty about the marriage in what looks like kindness. So they might say things like, "*I know that I have it all and you're wonderful...but it just isn't enough. It just isn't making me happy and I don't know why.*"

Yet regardless of which approach he takes, the purpose is often the same. To put himself in a position where he can indulge himself and do what he wants, and you have to basically go along with it until he figures himself out, or figures out what he wants. After all, you're a loving and supportive wife, right? That's what marriage is all about, right?

I hope this gives you some insight into why a husband who is going through a midlife crisis may say things like "*I don't know what I want*" or "*I don't know how I feel about you*" and why he might act confused or uncertain about his commitment to your marriage.

But how do you deal with it? I've already advised you how *not* to deal with it.

The Shut-Out Wife

That means not asking him a barrage of questions he can't or won't answer, something that only reinforces his position of power and puts you in a subordinate position. Plus, you're just not going to get any answers, and that's only going to add to your confusion, stress and heartache.

So don't react like this. In fact, don't *react* at all.

Respond instead. I'll share an example of what I mean.

A while back, I was working with a woman whose husband was doing this stuff quite badly—saying he wasn't sure what he wanted, didn't know if he felt passion for her, wasn't sure if he wanted to be married, etc.

Moreover, he kind of fluctuated between saying this in mean ways and saying it in what sounded like kinder ways.

So sometimes the message was hard—*"I'm just not attracted to you anymore and I don't know if I ever will be again"* and sometimes the message was softer—*"I know you're amazing, but I don't know if I want to be married anymore...I don't know if I can be happy here...it's not you, it's me."*

Mixed messages? You'd better believe it.

Of course, she would start asking him questions. *"What can I do? What would make you happy? What is making you unhappy?"* And of course, he either couldn't or wouldn't answer these questions.

She described a situation to me where this had been going on for over three months. It had become something of an expected interaction, a habitual way of communicating.

So I challenged her to try something different. I said, next time he says he *"doesn't know"* what he wants, I want you to respond in a similar way.

Instead of making it all about him, instead of giving him all the power, maybe it's time to take back some of the spotlight. To take back some power.

So she tried it. The next time he said he didn't know what he wanted, she simply shrugged and said, "*Well, to be brutally honest, I don't know what I want anymore, either. All of this has given me a lot to think about. It's changed our marriage and the way I feel about it.*"

And then she walked away. Not ignorantly. Not spitefully. She just went off and did something else.

This approach has a few benefits.

First, it prevents a wife from descending into that bottomless pit of unanswered questions, and all of the frustration, anxiety and hurt that goes along with that.

Second, it takes the husband off guard and shows him that it isn't all about him. He doesn't have all the power here, even though he might think he does.

As you know, a spouse who is having a serious midlife crisis can be profoundly self-focused. He expects the world to revolve around his feelings and confusion, his journey of self- rediscovery. It's all about him. He fully expects his wife to stick by him through all of this: in fact, she might have even told him that she would. Many wives will say things like, "*I'll be here no matter what to support you. I'm committed to our marriage no matter what.*"

In some circumstances, that's the right message to send. In others, in those situations that have escalated to long-term indecision and self-focus, it may not be as appropriate.

When this wife sent a different message, when she said, "*I don't know what I want anymore, either*" she took some of that focus off of him. She took some of her power back.

She burst his bubble by letting him know that she has a mind of her own and she's going through her own thought processes. And he probably wasn't ready for that. That's because some midlife men are so self-focused that it doesn't even occur to them that their wife would possibly tire of their behavior and actually decide to end the marriage. They just assume that if the marriage ends, they'll be the one who decides to end it.

The third benefit of this approach is that it actually can prompt a wife to empower herself and to start thinking and behaving in the ways that are in her best interests. It can make her realize that she *does* have a voice in all of this.

She does not have to be at the mercy of her husband's words, she does not have to be at the mercy of his decisions or behavior. She can think clearly and critically about what is happening, she can control her emotions, and she can make her own decisions.

To tell you the truth, out of everything I can convey in this book, that is the single most important lesson you can learn. You are not powerless in all of this.

Now, a final thought in this section. A reminder, really.

Remember that your husband may indeed be truly confused or uncertain about his feelings for you and his commitment to the marriage. That's why in part one I encouraged you to be supportive and understanding, to acknowledge your own shortcomings and to work with him to resolve past issues and create a better future.

But his need for happiness or to decide what he wants is not more important than your need to feel loved, secure, respected and happy. The real problem with male midlife crises that escalate is that the husband's needs end up outweighing and sometimes obliterating the wife's needs. Marriage is a partnership, a balancing act. And if it's all about him and his needs, at the serious expense of yours, then the balance is off.

If He Doesn't Know What He Wants, Should You Put a Deadline on His Indecision?

Another case I'd like mention at this point involved a client whose midlife husband was doing this sort of thing—expressing a lot of confusion about his feelings for her, and saying things like he "didn't know" what he wanted in life or what it would take for him to be happy, and so on.

The Shut-Out Wife

He would routinely go online to search for vacant apartments, although he didn't actually rent one. He'd talk about how he needed his space and he'd leave the computer on so that his wife could see that he was looking through local apartment vacancies. But whenever she'd ask him if he had decided to move out, he's say, *"I don't know."*

As a result, she spent most of her days tiptoeing around him, afraid to push him over the edge. She'd cook his favorite meals, make herself available for sex whenever he wanted it, make sure the house was immaculate, make sure their teenage kids were quiet and didn't bother him, and so on.

He had a habit of staying out late, sometimes all night, but she was afraid to ask him where he'd been—because if she did ask, he'd say she was controlling and was smothering him.

So as you can see, by keeping her in the "I don't know what I want" zone, he had created a pretty nice set up for himself—home-cooked meals, sexual fulfillment, a clean and quiet house, and he could come and go as he liked, with no questions asked of him and no demands put on him.

This lady spent the better part of six months living like this. Things hit a crisis point for her when she discovered that he'd been looking through dating sites.

If I had to guess, I'd say this man was laying that foundation that I talked about—because if he "didn't know" how he felt about his wife and marriage, who could blame him for exploring his feelings by dating other women? I mean, that's just the logical thing to do, right? Of course not, and when I say it like that, I'm sure you can see just how absurd it is. It's a very self-serving rationalization. Nonetheless, many wives fall into the trap of believing this. We'll chalk that up to the fear and confusion they feel.

In any event, I'll go into more detail about extramarital affairs in part three. For now, I just want to share with you how this wife handled things when she first discovered her husband was looking through dating sites.

First, she knew that was an absolute deal-breaker for her. He had cheated on her years previously, and she swore to herself she would never go through it again. And she meant it.

So she called me and we talked and brainstormed, and we came up with some different ways she could handle the situation. This is what she ultimately chose to say and do.

She did not mention that she'd come across the dating sites he'd been on. As she and I discussed, that would likely be pointless. He'd probably accuse her of being controlling and of violating his privacy and so on—those were accusations he usually made when she asked him about something—so it would just lead to a fight.

Plus, he knew he shouldn't be on those sites and had sworn he'd stay off them after his previous infidelity...so again, other than chastising him like a child, there was just no point in telling him. He'd find a way to deflect or blame her, and she'd end up scolding him like she was his mother and they'd have a fight. All pointless. And all things that she swore she wouldn't go through again.

Instead, she waited for him to create an opening. She was washing up the dishes after supper when he started to pack up his gym bag.

She said, *"Oh, you're heading to the gym?"*

Right away, he tensed up—that was his go-to way of telling her not to proceed—and nodded.

But she kept going and politely asked a very reasonable question: *"Are you coming home tonight?"*

At that, he sighed heavily. Again, his way of telling her that she was walking on forbidden ground.

"I don't know yet what I'm doing," he said.

"Well, I know what I'm doing," she said. *"I'm bringing some certainty to my life. I have an appointment with a lawyer for two weeks from today. If you can't commit to this marriage 100% by then, I'll be filing for divorce. I love you but I've been living like this for months and I need to move forward."*

Of course, her husband reacted as she knew he would. He accused her of pressuring him, of not giving him space, he said she was a very selfish person for giving him an ultimatum and it just proved how little she cared about the marriage, and so on.

And I have to give her credit. Despite feeling that strong urge to react to those accusations and to defend herself, she didn't fall into his trap—she knew exactly what he was trying to do. He was trying to deflect everything away from his own behavior and pin it on her. So instead of reacting out of anger or emotion, she responded.

She simply said, *"We're both entitled to the way we see things right now and we're both able to make the choices that we feel are in our best interests."*

And then she told him to have a good workout at the gym and continued to wash up the dishes.

As the days went by, she stuck to her guns. No arguing, no defending, no explaining—and her husband really upped the ante. He stayed away for three nights in a row and again, she knew why. He was trying to scare her and intimate her into backing down.

When she didn't back down, he made a point of leaving his computer screen on to show that he'd been visiting divorce lawyers' websites. On top of that, he made sure that she could overhear conversations he was having with friends and family, where he was complaining that she was kicking him out and not willing to work on the marriage anymore.

Yet she was determined to keep her focus and her clarity. She knew what he was doing and why, so she didn't react to it.

She didn't get mad, she didn't repeat or explain herself, she didn't defend what she was doing.

Instead, she remained clear and respectful at all times. She respected herself and she respected her husband, even if his behavior wasn't respectful toward her.

As the two-week deadline closed in, she didn't once remind him of that date or ask him if he'd managed to find clarity about their marriage. Her appointment was booked for one o'clock in the afternoon. That morning, her husband got up and had breakfast with her. She could tell he was wondering, but she didn't say anything.

Finally, he asked. *"Are you going to that lawyer today?"*

"Yes I am," she said as respectfully as she could.

"So you're done with our marriage, then?" he asked.

"I've said my piece and you know where I stand," she said.

Again, she knew what he was doing. He was trying to deflect, to engage her in a dialogue and put her on the defensive. He was looking for a way to buy some time and avoid having to make a decision.

I'll fast-forward what happened in this case. He said nothing, and she kept the appointment. She went to the lawyer and she started the process of a separation. When she got home, her husband was still sitting at the kitchen table.

"I'd like to give our marriage another try," he said.

"Okay," she said. *"But it has to work for both of us. I won't do all the work. You know what you have to do, so either you're going to do it, or you aren't. No more questions, no more reminders, no more warnings. Either it works for me, or it doesn't."*

And then do you know what she did? She made herself a cup of coffee, gave her husband an affectionate squeeze on the shoulder and went into her office to work on some files.

Yes, He "Gets It"

The hardest thing about this approach, and the other approaches I've offered, is that a woman often thinks her husband doesn't "get it." She thinks he doesn't "get" what she's doing or why she's doing it, or what the consequences might be.

The Shut-Out Wife

She fears that if she doesn't constantly explain herself, or sell herself, or defend herself, he will misunderstand what she's doing (say, shrugging it off and walking away) and leave her once and for all.

Similarly, she fears that if she doesn't constantly convince him to stay, if she doesn't cling to him, he will just drift away. She fears that if she relaxes at all and lets go of him, she'll lose whatever grip she had and he'll walk away.

This woman had those fears: she feared that if she stepped back and didn't say anything, if she didn't remind him of the lawyer's appointment, he would forget about it, and she'd be in a position of filing for divorce…and she feared he would not take any steps to stop that from happening.

But she faced that fear. She knew, deep down, that she had no control over whether he left or not—and she chose to take *real* control of her own life by letting go of that *illusion* of control.

She knew, deep down, that her husband knew exactly how he had been mistreating her and how self-focused he had become. He knew all her complaints and he knew how she wanted him to behave. He already knew how to be a good, loving and devoted husband. There was no reason for her to teach him how to do that.

Neither did she need to warn him against having another affair. That's because he knew, full well, that he was a married man and being intimate with another woman was wrong. There was no reason for her to mention this. He was either going to have an affair or he wasn't. She had no more control over that happening again than she did the first time it happened.

Of course, it took every ounce of self-discipline she could muster to stay level when he made his big announcement—that he wanted to give their marriage another try. If he had been expecting her to burst into tears of gratitude or drop to her knees in relief, he was disappointed.

Instead, her response was measured, clear and confident. She remained in control of herself and of the situation. That's what you have to do.

Now, this strategy—putting a deadline on your husband's state of indecision or uncertainty—isn't suited to all cases.

Not all men use indecisiveness or uncertainty as a way to buy time or indulge themselves. Some men are *truly* conflicted or unsure about what they want—that is especially so if there have been serious or long-standing problems in the marriage. That is especially so if your husband has legitimate complaints about you or your behavior. Again, that is why working through part one is so important. You must be honest and accountable for your own mistakes or poor behavior. You deserve to be happy and be with a partner who makes you happy—but so does your husband.

There are also situations where a wife probably doesn't want to give her husband the heads-up that she's thinking of ending the marriage or seeing a lawyer. That may be the case if she suspects he's seeing another woman and possibly spending money on this person. If things are really bad, a wife may wish to consult a lawyer and protect her financial interests before she vocalizes a deadline for the marriage. A word to the wise will suffice here.

But in this case, this woman did decide it was the best approach for her. She had been living this way for months and felt in her heart that she had done everything she could on her end. She didn't hold out much hope that her husband would step up. She was fairly certain that he was on the verge of cheating on her again, if he hadn't already, and she couldn't live with the anxiety of his constant confusion and uncertainty anymore.

Basically, this woman needed to make a change for own emotional well-being. And since she'd tried just about everything else that both of us could think of, this was kind of a last resort for her. The way she saw it, she had nothing to lose at that point.

So overall, if you believe your husband's behavior is self-serving and unfair, and if have protected your own interests, putting a deadline on his state of indecision or uncertainty can be a good strategy, one that can give you a much-needed sense of certainty in your life.

But again, it does involve your relinquishing that illusion of control. In the end, you must accept that your husband is a grown man who knows what he is doing, and knows—or should know—what he is doing to you.

He "gets it." Ultimately, he will do what he wants with his own life, and he will act in his best interests, whether that means staying, going, getting help, whatever. So for once, I suggest that you follow his lead.

When (and Why) He Says, "I love you, but I'm not *in love* with you."

"I love you, but I'm not in love with you."

This is a classic statement made by a man in the throes of a self-focused midlife episode. And a wife who hears it has probably never felt such pain, panic and confusion in her entire life. It can be a devastating thing to hear, one that can chip away at a woman's sense of security, self-worth and well-being. As with so many statements said by a midlife man, this one can have shades of truth, or it can be completely self-serving.

Is it possible that a man who makes this statement really isn't in love with his wife anymore, despite the years they've been together, despite their children and history? Yes, it's possible. The question is whether he has truly fallen out of love or whether he has simply lost feelings of passion for his wife. That is, is this a permanent state or a temporary one?

It's common for married people, whether they're going through a midlife crisis or not, to lose feelings of passionate love. They're a long way from the lust and excitement and infatuation phases of a long-term partnership. Things are familiar, maybe even boring.

People in midlife often long to feel the "buzz" of being alive. And if a husband isn't feeling electric passion for his wife, he makes this distinction between loving her and being "in love" with her. So the statement may have shades of truth to it, at least that version of the truth that your husband chooses to believe right now.

Yet that statement can also be purely self-indulgent and self-serving. "*I love you, but I'm not in love with you.*" As we've seen, a man (or a woman, for that matter!) might say this to justify an extramarital affair, either one he's currently having or one that he's thinking about having. A spouse might argue that it isn't actually cheating if he isn't in love with his wife anymore.

Of course it isn't true. As long as you're married, it's cheating. That's the truth, although it's a truth that people have to bend if they want to justify an affair.

That statement—"*I love you, but I'm not in love with you*"—may be confusing to a wife, but the translation is really pretty simple. It means something like this: *We have a long history together, but I don't feel passion for you right now.*

So...what do you do about this? How do you handle this?

Well, you've read enough of this book to know how not to handle it. The last thing you want to do is start arguing with him or lecturing him about how he can't expect his feelings of passion to be as strong now as they were in the beginning of your relationship, or at least during the times when you were happier.

Don't sell yourself like that! It comes across as desperate. Plus, he already knows this. Every married person knows this. If you argue, he will only defend what he is saying, and in the process, his feelings toward you will become even more negative.

Similarly, it's probably pointless to ask him to explain what he means by that, or to try to convince him that he's wrong. Again, it's likely going to end in an argument as he defends his position and, in process, begins to feel even less love for you.

I understand this is an excruciating thing to hear from the man you love, but I urge you to question the wisdom of letting your emotions—your panic, fear or anger—get the better of you. I urge you to not react out of pure, raw emotion. I urge you to avoid falling into a reactive state where you fly at him with questions or you rage or cry or beg, or where you try to persuade him to feel different.

All of those reactions keep the focus squarely and exclusively on him. It's all about his feelings or lack of feelings. If he's already acting in self-focused ways, the last thing you want to do is add to that sense that it's all about him.

Instead, I suggest you do three things.

First, keep your emotions in check. Stay in control of yourself. Don't break down into tears, don't rage at him. Don't let that statement turn you into a reactive puddle of emotion.

Second, respond to his statement in a way that takes the focus off of him. For example, you might say something like, *"I've felt that way about you at times, too."* And leave it there.

Don't ask him what he's going to do—*"Are you going to leave me? Are you going to move out? If you don't love me, does that mean you're going to file for divorce?"*

There's no point asking these questions. In all likelihood, he'll only answer by saying he doesn't know. Accept that he's going to do what he's going to do. Let him make the next move, then at least you'll know what you're dealing with.

The chances are very good that your husband will not be expecting this kind of measured, restrained response from you. He may not expect to hear that you've felt that way about him at times, too. As we've seen, some midlife men can become quite egocentric. The last thing you want to do is feed that ego any more.

You don't want to rip him apart or insult him, but you do want to send the message, respectfully, that he isn't the center of the world, even if he assumes he is. That's the only way you're going to have a voice and keep some power.

That statement "*I love you, but I'm not in love with you,*" has a kind of apocalyptic feel to it, doesn't it? It sounds like the marriage is over, doesn't it?

But when you keep your emotions in check, when you keep some power for yourself, you deflate the apocalyptic feel of that statement.

When you don't freak out or fall apart at the words, you strip them of their meaning and impact. He can and will make whatever statement he wants, but you don't need to validate it. You can just let his words dissolve into the air. They're just sounds.

Now, the third way to respond is a more positive, proactive way. There's no doubt that feelings of being in love with our spouse can come and go. They are weaker and stronger at different points in our marriage. There's an old saying: a successful marriage means falling in love many times, and always with the same person...

So if you hear those words from your husband—I love you but I'm not in love with you—you're wise to think about the first two strategies I mentioned. Keep your emotions in check and let him know that you've felt the same way at times. Let him feel heard, but don't make it all about him.

But at the same time, you have to accept that he may truly feel this way right now. Therefore, I have a few questions for you to ponder:

- When you look back, when did you feel the most love from your husband?

- When you look back, when do you think he felt the most love from you?

- When you look back, when do you think you were the happiest as a couple?

When you have a good picture of that time in your mind, I want you to think about what kind of wife you were then. How did you communicate or interact with your husband? Were you more affectionate, supportive, fun, playful or interesting?

Basically, I want you to rediscover some of the things that he used to love about you, and to start doing those again. I know that easier said than done right now, especially if you've heard these words. And I want to be clear—I am not saying that I want you to accept responsibility for everything, or that I want you to throw yourself at him.

What I am saying is that most long-term partners change over time. We drop the ball a bit when it comes to the way we communicate or interact with our partner. And it's always wise now and then to stop, and think. Am I still that person my spouse fell in love with? I know this is the kind of thing I talked about in part one, but it's worth repeating here.

As your husband's behavior continues to escalate, you definitely have to take measures to protect yourself from his increasing self-focus and self-serving statements, attitude and behavior. You need to take the hardline at times, letting him know that it isn't all about him.

But even as you're doing that, you can still take proactive steps to address any legitimate complaints he may have about you.

So if you hear those dreaded words—I love you, but I'm not in love with you—think about the three strategies I've outlined here.

Instead of arguing or pleading or panicking, keep your emotions in check. Instead of adding to his self-focus, let him know that you've felt the same way at times. It isn't all about him.

And while you do these things, ask yourself: When did my husband seem the most "in love" with me? When were we the happiest as a couple? Are there behaviors or personality traits that I can reclaim, not just to make him happy, but also to be happier person myself?

Should You Keep Having Sex With Him?

As I've said, that statement—"*I love you, but I'm not in love with you*"—can be a true reflection of a man's uncertainty or confusion about his marriage and how he feels about his wife. If you believe that's the case with you, I suggest you revisit part one of this book and see how you can reach him.

This statement can also be part of a larger way of thinking on his part. He might say it as a way to justify an affair or moving out, or as a way to distance himself from his feelings for you.

Yet it's always surprising to me how many men will say something along these lines to their wife and yet fully expect to keep sleeping in the same bed and even having sex with her.

When this happens, a wife is typically baffled. *"He says he isn't in love with me, yet he's still in our bed. He still wants to have sex with me. So doesn't that mean he loves me?"*

When you hear those words—I love you, but I'm not in love with you—or when you hear a similar sentiment, it is my strong opinion that you need to immediately put limits on both emotional and sexual intimacy. No being his confidant or sounding board. And definitely no sex.

As you know, the choices you make are ultimately up to you. You're the real expert in your marriage and nobody knows your husband like you do. But all else being equal, I disagree with the advice some coaches and counselors give—which is to keep sleeping with him to maintain some kind of intimacy. The way I see it, this sends a husband a problematic message.

It says to him: *You can say anything you want to me, even something heart-breaking, and I will still give you my heart, soul and body whenever you want it. I am willing to have sex with you, even if you aren't sure that you love me....because you're that amazing and I'm that desperate. Even if your commitment to the marriage is uncertain, mine is so absolute that I am here to pleasure you whenever you want me to.*

To me, that is not intimacy at all. That's just one person getting to have an orgasm whenever they feel like it, and the other person living in anguish.

In my opinion, this strips a woman not just of her personal power in the marriage, but also of her dignity. And her husband sees that. He sees just how much power he has—sole power—and he realizes that he has a license to do and say whatever he wants.

In my opinion, there is nothing to be gained from sharing your heart or your body with a man who says he doesn't love you, or who has qualified the love he feels for you. I cannot think of a more soul-sucking experience.

I understand that you want to feel reassured that he loves you. You may think that having sex with him will rekindle his love for you. That's unlikely. I mean, you've had sex with him for years, perhaps even decades, and he has still drifted away.

To be brutally honest, if he does have sex with you, it may be more of a maintenance thing for him rather than an act of devoted love. He's going to turn over and go to sleep or get up, get dressed and get going.

Meanwhile, you may be left to deal with the emotional fallout. You may be left to wonder what it all meant, alternating between feelings of hope and loss. During lovemaking, you may feel connected, or that you are reaching him—but are you, really?

Only you can answer that question, but I think it is unlikely. In too many situations, a woman has sex with him out of hope that it will flip some kind of switch and he'll fall back in love and recommit to her. Ask yourself honestly—is that why you're doing it? And if so, has it worked?

Remember, your husband is the one who has changed the parameters of your marriage and the nature of your relationship. He has indicated that he does not feel passionate love for you, or he has in some way qualified his love for you.

That is a significant change in the nature of your life together, and you need to adapt to that change. Those are strong words to speak to one's spouse. He knows what he said. Now he needs to know that those words have consequences.

When (and Why) He Acts Hot & Cold: Dealing with Mixed Messages

Men who are going through a serious midlife crisis are famous for sending mixed messages. One minute, he's talking about how unhappy he is, how he's never really been happy in the marriage and how he's never really felt passionate love for you. The next minute, he's telling you you're beautiful and initiating sex.

One minute he's talking about how he wants to move out of the house and get a divorce. The next minute he's planning a vacation for the two of you. One minute he's kind and affectionate, the next he's cruel and distant.

For his wife, it's like living life in an emotional blender. There are periods of calm where things settle, and then it all gets whipped up into a storm of pain and confusion.

Generally speaking, there are a few overarching reasons that a midlife man sends mixed messages to his wife. The first is because he's indulging his ever-changing emotions and whims.

If he feels nostalgic about the marriage, he is loving to his wife. If he feels irritated by her or attracted to another woman, he is critical and cold to her. One day he may feel that he wants to remain in the marriage and work on it. So that's the message he sends his wife, and she feels reassured and hopeful. The next day, he's changed his mind. He wants out. So that's the message he sends his wife, and she feels devastated and shattered. The messages are mixed.

As you may already know, a spouse in the throes of a midlife crisis can be a very moody person. His emotions and thoughts can be scattered and inconsistent, and his behavior can be impulsive and unpredictable. And if he refuses to restrain that kind of impulsiveness, if he chooses to give in to it and just behave in whatever way the wind blows him, his wife is left blowing in the wind, too.

A second reason that a midlife man sends mixed messages is perhaps a more strategic and purposeful one. He actually wants to keep his wife in a state of confusion. He knows he's sending her mixed messages and he knows why. Because it keeps her guessing. It keeps her walking on eggshells. It makes her afraid to put any demands on him or to express her own needs. In this situation, a woman can never quite find her footing. As soon as she does, as soon as she starts to think she has some stability, he pulls the rug out from under her with another mixed message.

A third reason that a midlife man sends mixed messages is to avoid being accountable for what he says or does. He can use his changing moods and emotions as a way to justify whatever he does or doesn't do. *"Well, I wasn't feeling in love with you at that time...that's why I slept with someone else...but now I do feel love for you, so I'm willing to be faithful."*

He can also use his mixed messages as a safety net. As a way of keeping his options open. If one day he says he wants a divorce, but the next day he says he doesn't, well, he can safely choose either option.

So those are a few of the main reasons for mixed messages. They're either self-indulgent and indifferent to / unaware of the emotional turmoil they put you through, or they're strategic and purposeful. You know your husband best, and you know what has been transpiring during this midlife crisis episode—that means you probably know, in your heart, his reasons for sending them.

But how do you handle his mixed messages? Let's look at a few scenarios.

Let's say a midlife man has been sending his wife mixed messages about his commitment level to the marriage. One minute he's devoted to making it work, the next he's out the door. His wife, like most of us, might instinctively react to this by getting angry, asking questions or begging him to stay and work on it.

She might question him: *"Why do you want to leave today? Yesterday you wanted to stay. What's changed? What can I do?"*

Of course, she won't get any answers to these questions...at least not any reliable or meaningful answers. So instead, I suggest not asking any questions. I also suggest not putting too much stock into anything he says, whether it's good or bad.

Instead, it might be better to remain emotionally non-reactive. Stay calm in the face of his storm. Do not let his mixed messages constantly swing you from feelings of hope and reassurance to feelings of despair and pain. Do not indulge his changing emotions or whims.

If he says something positive—*"I want to work on the marriage"*—simply say, *"That's good to hear."*

If he says, *"You're so beautiful,"* simply say, *"Thank you."*

And then do your very best to not put too much hope or trust in that. Keep those feelings of hope and trust in check—you must in order to protect yourself.

If he says something negative—*"I'm done here!"*—simply say, *"I understand."*

If he says, *"I can't stay in this house one more night,"* simply say, *"Okay."*

If he says something mean or insulting, simply say, *"That's rude,"* and walk away.

Remember—when he says something mean or insulting, it isn't about you, it's about him. It's about his agenda. So do not put too much stock into anything he says.

I often advise women who are receiving extreme mixed-messages from their midlife husbands, and who have exhausted the strategies in part one of this book, to emotionally disconnect from his words. Easier said than done, right? But it has to happen.

Do not pin your hopes onto his sweet messages. Do not sink into despair when he sends a painful message.

Think of his words as just sounds, just noises. The only meaning they have is the meaning you allow them to have. The only power they have is the power that you give them.

How to Deal with His Meanness and/or Moodiness

Make no mistake—many spouses in the throes of a self-indulgent midlife crisis test the waters by seeing how much they can get away with. They want to know how poorly they can speak to or treat their wife. They want to know how far they can indulge their own moods and desires before she's had enough and either leaves or asks him to leave.

Many times during my years in practice I've been surprised and dismayed by just how mean and moody a midlife man can be to his wife.

Wives have told me that their husbands have said things like, *"Your body changed when you turned forty. It's hard for me to feel visually turned on by you."*

Sometimes, these things were even said in a professional's office under the pretense of "being honest."

So why does he do it? There are a number of reasons. He may simply be indulging his own self-grandeur and ever-changing thoughts and whims. If he has a nasty thought about you, he has no filter, no empathy, and no respect. He just blurts it out. He may have a narcissistic streak. Or, as I recently said, he may be testing the waters. He may want to see how much he can get away with.

He might also want you to believe it so that you feel you have no better option but to remain with him. After all, if he can convince you that you're too undesirable to have any value, then he can strip you of your personal power and options. As the more youthful, sexier and smarter spouse, he's in control and you're easier to manage.

He might also be saying these mean things to convince himself that you're an unappealing partner. He wants to write a story, a narrative, where you're the antagonist and he's the good guy, and because of that, he is justified in doing what he's doing.

But for that story to be written, you have to play your part. He needs you to believe what he says—that you're unattractive, or whatever. That, or he needs you to argue, to fly into a rage, to call him names and to validate what he's saying by your ugly behavior. So he says something mean or slips into a nasty mood, knowing full well that you're going to react to it. I mean, who wouldn't? And when you do, you complete his narrative.

So how do you handle it? Well, you don't play the part he's trying to pin on you. You don't let him convince you that you're unappealing or undesirable or unworthy of him. You don't buy what he's selling.

Make no mistake—whatever mean message he's trying to send says a lot more about *him* and his agenda than it does about you!

If he says something mean or insulting, resist the urge to react instinctively or defensively. That only feeds his narrative.

Instead, simply say, "That's rude," and walk away. Make it about him and his rude behavior, not about you. Treat him the same way you'd treat anyone else who said something mean or insulting to you. Show him, through your refusal to acknowledge or engage, that his words have no power over you.

Picture this: You're walking down the street when a grown man you don't know yells, *"Hey lady, catch this!"* and then throws a big stick covered in mud at you. What do you do? Do you try to catch it? Do you just stand there and let it hit you, and ruin your good jacket?

Of course not. You move aside. You let the muddy stick land on the ground. You don't try to catch it or dig through the thistles to find it if it lands in the bushes. You just leave it on the ground, infused as it is with that person's anger or rudeness.

Well, when someone, including your spouse, says something mean to you, you don't have to catch it, either. You don't have to just stand there and let those words cover you in mud. You can step aside and let the whole message just fall flat on the ground.

Now let's continue with this little metaphor. After this muddy stick has landed on the ground, do you continue to stand on the sidewalk and argue with the grown man who threw it at you? Do you launch into a long explanation about how hurtful his behavior was? Do you ask him why he threw it? Do you start chastising him for throwing it?

You might be tempted to do these things, but you know that would only escalate the situation. If he was a thoughtful gentleman who cared about your feelings in that moment, he wouldn't have thrown a muddy stick at you in the first place.

It's a similar thing with a spouse in the throes of a self-indulgent midlife episode. It isn't your job to chastise a grown man—even one you married!—in the way you would chastise a child. It isn't your job to convince a grown man that it's wrong to say mean things. It isn't your job to explain basic human courtesy to him.

He knows the difference between right and wrong. He knows the meaning of the words he's chosen to speak to you. It's on him, not you. He "gets it."

Again, this is an area where my approach differs from some other practitioners. I've had clients who had, before seeing me, been advised to keep telling their husband just how disrespectful and hurtful his words were.

The advice was something like this: *"Every time he says something mean or hurtful to you, tell him it was mean or hurtful...tell him how it made you feel."*

But when I asked my clients how that approach worked, they usually said that it didn't work. They usually said that their husband either argued with them, blamed them or somehow justified what he was saying.

They also said that their husband continued to say mean things, no matter how many times they told him it was disrespectful, hurtful, et cetera.

So really, we're back to that basic approach. Shrug it off and walk away. If you're sitting on the couch watching TV and he says something mean, get up and go for a walk. If you're in a restaurant and he says something mean, get up and go home.

Is it a perfect response? Maybe, maybe not. It's hard to find a perfect response to anything done or said by a person in the throes of a self-focused midlife crisis. There are just so many variables and unknowns. Sometimes it just comes down to the least bad response.

Here, as with many of my suggestions, it comes down to setting limits to protect your emotional, mental and physical well-being. It comes down to showing him—through your actions, not just your words—that he simply cannot mistreat or disrespect you. This is his issue and he needs to deal with it.

Remember that. This is his midlife episode. Yes, he's your husband and you need to understand and support him. But if you've done everything you can on your end and his behavior continues to escalate, you simply cannot allow his crisis to become your crisis.

You're Not His Counselor – So Don't Act Like it!

As a lot of us already know, midlife is a time of reflection and transition. Things are changing. Our family dynamics might be changing with kids growing up and leaving. Our bodies are changing. Our priorities, minds, and hearts, might be changing, too.

All of this is okay and very natural. We all need to slow down and put conscious thought into what isn't working or hasn't worked in our lives, and into what has worked. We need to think about the things that have prevented us from being happy, and we need to make changes.

We need to embrace the gifts of middle age—the freedom to be ourselves, to re-discover or to re-create ourselves. "Know thyself." It's a Delphic maxim. Socrates said, *"The unexamined life is not worth living."* People and powers greater than us have extolled the virtues of a thoughtful life. Of self-analysis.

Yet many women who find themselves faced with a husband's unusual or alarming behavior during a midlife episode fall back into a very female way of responding—they start to analyze their husband!

They put all their energy and focus into scrutinizing him, his motives, his character, his behavior, his needs and desires. They come up with all kinds of theories and ideas about why he's doing what he's doing. Maybe he has a brain tumor, maybe his hormones are changing, maybe he had a bad childhood.

Now, to some extent, that type of scrutinizing and desire to understand is appropriate. Of course we need to support our spouse through hard times. Of course we need to be patient, empathetic, forgiving and loving, and of course we need to help them figure out life's challenges. That's something I encouraged you to do in part one. But there has to be a limit to that, and that limit often depends on how our spouse responds to our efforts.

Here in part two, we're talking about situations where a midlife spouse has—in one way or many ways—rejected his wife's attempts to understand and help him. We're talking about situations where a midlife spouse's behavior has escalated to the point that it is negatively impacting his wife's well-being and quality of life, and threatening the stability of the marriage.

And when a wife gets to this point, it may be time to stop analyzing her husband. It may be time to stop diagnosing his problems or telling him what she thinks is wrong or suggesting solutions. He probably isn't listening anyway. That is, it may be time for her to stop acting like her husband's personal counselor.

If a wife doesn't do this, if she continues to live her life in a state of constant analysis, she reinforces her husband's self-focus and self-indulgence. She keeps the spotlight on him. And in the process, she just kind of disappears into the darkness.

Yes, your husband may be going through a lot of emotional, physical and spiritual turmoil. I suspect you are, too. Yes, his choices and behaviors may be putting a strain on his relationships—not just his relationship with you, but also with his children or siblings or parents or friends or co-workers.

But it is not your job to counsel him into perpetuity at the cost of your own happiness and peace of mind. It is not your job to diagnose or treat or fix him. It is not your job to serve as his personal talk therapist. It is not your job to turn into a family mediator who must exhaust herself trying to make him maintain a quality relationship with his children. It may hurt to see that relationship falter, especially if the kids feel it. That's why you need to be there for them. Save your energy for them. Don't waste it trying to mediate or convince your husband to see his children. He knows their names, he knows where they live, he knows how to contact them, he knows how to behave around them.

What he does with that knowledge is up to him. It is not your responsibility. You are not a bad mother for doing this!

I encourage you to think twice about exhausting your emotional, physical, mental and spiritual energy trying to analyze your husband. Do not put your own life on hold until he figures out what he wants to do with his.

He's an adult man who, in all likelihood is continuing to function in other areas of his life, at least those areas that he feels are important to him—he's eating, drinking, refueling his car, and putting in the effort to maintain those relationships he is choosing to prioritize (even if, unfortunately, that isn't his wife).

I've had more than one unhappy wife say words to this effect: *"He is sweet as pie on the phone when he's talking to his mother / co-worker / whomever, but as soon as he hangs up, he's rude to me."* Or: *"He can spend two hours working out, but he can't spare ten minutes to go for a walk with me?"* Or: *"He's all smiles when we're chatting with the neighbor or with company, but the moment we're alone, he's all scowls again."*

Even if your husband is going through an authentic midlife episode where he is reevaluating his life and full of conflicting emotions, even if he is making some poor choices, it is still his responsibility to take care of himself and to make adult decisions…to receive the care he needs from those who are offering to help him. His issue does not give him carte blanche to unleash meanness, confusion and pain onto you.

And—I'll say it yet again—this is why part one of this book is so important. You need to be sure you've been fair to and supportive of him…beyond that, all of us, as adults, need to take responsibility for ourselves.

That often means stepping back, and not always being his self-appointed counselor or shoulder to cry on. You are not abandoning him by doing this. You can only do what you can do. He knows he can come to you if and when he is ready to truly face what is happening and work through it with you.

Stay On-Track with this Trio of Truths

I've worked with many wives who are enduring months of a husband's self-focused midlife episode. And one of the most frustrating things for me is when I go through these various insights and strategies and a wife responds by saying, *"I know I should do some of these things, but I just want him to listen!"* or *"I just want him to see what he's doing!"* or *"But I love him!"*

You know what? I want you to love *yourself*. You hear that so often it's become trite—love yourself—but it's so very true. I want you to stop making excuses for him, or enabling him, or mothering him or trying to fix him, or trying to sell yourself to him! You will always be there for him if he is receptive to your help and love, and if he is respectful of you.

Do what you can. Do what is reasonable. Then pull back and ask yourself a question: "Do I feel confident that I've done everything I can on my end, but despite this, my husband is continuing to act in ways that are hurtful or disrespectful to me?"

If the answer is yes, I have a "trio of truths" that, despite their brevity and simplicity (or perhaps because of those!) might help you stay on track. That is, to stay on the track where you protect your own well-being and sanity, and stop falling into those pointless beating-your-head-against-a-wall thoughts and reactions.

What follows are three simple truths you can cling to when you feel tempted to *succumb* to his mixed messages, or to *ask questions* he won't answer, or to pointlessly *argue or debate* him, or to *repeat yourself* (yet again!), or to *persuade* him to come back, or to *explain* to him how he's hurting you, or to *convince* him that he's wrong to treat you poorly, or to *plead* with him to listen to you, or to *warn* him that he's making a mistake, or to excessively and endlessly *analyze* his every move and word...

Free yourself of those knee-jerk, self-sabotaging and never-ending reactions by remembering:

Truth # 1. Your husband is a grown man

Truth # 2. Your husband is fully aware of his behavior toward you, and why you are responding the way you are (that is, he "gets it")

Truth # 3. Your husband is the only person in the world who can choose to change his behavior (that is, you can't force or persuade or compel or guilt him into doing it)

Accept this trio of truth: he's a grown man, he knows what he's doing, and only he can choose to change or ask for help. If and when you can accept these truths, you can liberate yourself. You can free yourself from that constant state of uncertainty, and anxiety, and speculation and waiting—always, always waiting!—for some change or some sign from him.

If and when that comes, he must be the one who initiates it. If you're forever waiting on him, pursuing him, analyzing him, pleading with him to stay or getting into pointless arguments and dialogues—if you're doing that, you're out of control. He is in control. And he knows it. At some point, you need to take the focus off of him and put it back on yourself.

Make no mistake—the way you care for yourself during your husband's midlife crisis, the way you allow him to talk to you or treat you, will eventually be something that you will have to come to terms with on a personal level. That's why I'm constantly harping on you to empower yourself and to put thought into everything.

I've seen women come through their husband's midlife crisis and keep their marriages intact; however, once the dust settled, some were left with their husband's disrespectful or hurtful words ringing in their ears and, even worse, the memories of how they allowed that to continue for so long. They become angry with themselves and they bring that anger into the marriage.

That in turn can create a new set of problems. A husband often wants to quickly forget what happened and get on with life, but his wife may be left with some emotional bruises that take a little longer to heal and that require a little more care.

Oscar Wilde said that there are two tragedies in life: the first is not getting what want, and the other is getting it. If you want to keep your marriage intact and overcome this midlife episode, great. I only suggest that you remain aware of the toll that may be taking on you, and the toll it could take on the marriage in the future.

I'm not trying to discourage you here—there is every chance you will come out of this with a happy, even happier, marriage. To that end, I encourage you to remain in control of your own thoughts, emotions, behavior, and choices. Staying in control of yourself gives you the best shot of responding to this crisis instead of just reacting to it. That's how anyone survives any kind of crisis.

So as you go through the insights and strategies in this book, I hope that you will make clear-headed, conscious decisions regarding which ones you will choose to use, and how. In the end, you're the expert in your own marriage.

Even considering what's happening, you still know your husband and your situation best. With some objective thought and some new approaches at your disposal, you might learn to know him even better, and to teach him some important things about you in the process.

Q&A's, Part Two

The Big Picture

When you consider the six parts of a self-focused midlife crisis, do you see your spouse's behavior reflected therein? How so?

When you look at the "big picture" of his behavior, can you reasonably speculate on what he might do next?

When It's Totally Out of the Blue: The One-Part Midlife Episode

If you've previously felt that your husband's behavior came "out of the blue," is it possible that he was actually planning it for a while? Why do you think "yes" or "no"?

How to Deal With His Fitness / Appearance (or Other New) Obsession

Has your husband become obsessed with fitness? If so, how has this impacted the way he relates to you?

Can you "join in" his fitness effort, whether by joining his activity or by discovering your own unique way to become more active? List a few activities you might try:

If you feel criticized by your husband, how will you handle it moving forward? Jot down a few notes on how you **will** and **will not** respond to him.

When the "New Him" comes with an Inflated Ego

Make a note of whether and how your husband shows this kind of behavior, including what he tends to say or do.

Then write down how you **will not** respond to him (that is, write down the responses that usually backfire).

If your husband acts as though he is superior to you, how **will** you respond? Be prepared in advance, as this preparation will help you handle yourself in a calm, confident and collected way.

How to Handle his Self-Focus and Self-Indulgence

How can you disengage from his self-focus and self-indulgence in a way that lets you maintain your personal power and dignity?

Why You Need to Respond, Not React: Don't Be His Opponent!

To you, what is the difference between a reaction and a response? Can you think of an example?

Write down the ways you feel your husband may be trying to elicit a "reaction" out of you. Think about why he might be doing this, and how you can respond instead of react:

How does your husband tend to react when he feels you are taking back your power? How do you anticipate he might react when he sees this start to happen? And also, why do you think he might react in these ways?

If he reacts in a negative way, how do you plan on dealing with that?

How can you ensure that you don't inadvertently become his "opponent"?

When (and Why) He Sees You as the Problem

Why might your husband be blaming you for his unhappiness and/or problems in the marriage?

How should you **not** respond when he does this?

How can you maintain both your power and your dignity when your husband tries to blame you for "everything":

When (and Why) He Acts Confused or Unsure About the Marriage
(*"I don't know what I want"* or *"I need space"*)

How is your husband expressing confusion or uncertainty about his commitment to the marriage or his feelings for you?

Why might your husband be doing this? Is his indecisiveness authentic or do you feel it may be contrived to some extent to serve his interests? Are there elements of both?

Instead of focusing exclusively on meeting his needs or asking him what it will take to make him happy, how can you put the focus on both of you? How can you respectfully communicate to him that it isn't "all about him"?

If He Doesn't Know What He Wants,
Should You Put a Deadline on His Indecision?

If you feel that putting a deadline on your situation may help you, what might that deadline be?

Why are you choosing that time / date?
Are there any steps you need to take now, or to plan for, in case he does not recommit to you by the deadline?

Yes, He "Gets It"

Have you ever found yourself wondering whether your husband "gets it"? Try to think of a specific situation or interaction where you felt this way. How did it affect how you acted or responded to him?

If you instead assumed and accepted that he "gets it," might you have acted or responded in a different way? How so?

How might this acceptance change how you act or respond in the future? Try to imagine a scenario where you might remind yourself of this, and how you might proceed.

When (and Why) He Says, "I love you, but I'm not *in love* with you."

If your husband is expressing this or a similar sentiment, why do you think he is doing so?

When did your husband seem to love you the most? What was your life like then?

How did you speak to/interact with him at that time? How were you different?

Write down some ideas that might help you reclaim the happier aspects of your past:

Should You Keep Having Sex With Him?

If you are continuing to have sex with your husband despite his uncertainty about your marriage or his feelings for you, be honest with yourself: why are you doing so? What toll it is taking on you?

If you are continuing to have sex with your husband despite his uncertainty about your marriage or his feelings for you, ask yourself: what message is it sending him about himself and you?

Is it bringing you closer and making you more connected, or is it actually counterproductive? Only you can answer that question.

What are the pros and cons of continuing to have sex with him right now?

When (and Why) He Acts Hot & Cold: Dealing With Mixed Messages

What kinds of mixed messages is your husband sending you?

Why might he be sending you these mixed messages?

How are his mixed messages affecting you? How do they make you feel?

How should you **not** respond to his mixed messages?

Write down the more positive and effective ways you will deal with his mixed messages moving forward.

How to Deal with His Meanness and/or Moodiness

Why might he be behaving in mean or moody ways?

Is it possible you have been "playing a part he has written for you"? If so, how? And how might you stop doing that?

How will you deal with his meanness or moodiness moving forward? There may be no perfect solution, but what response best protects you?

Replay! Think back to an interaction between you and your husband, one that you felt went poorly. Now replay that, incorporating what you've learned so far—might you have been able to handle yourself, and the situation, better or differently?

You're Not His Counselor – So Don't Act Like It!

Have you been acting like his personal counselor or the family mediator? If so, how?

In what ways can you stop acting like his personal counselor or the family mediator?

How might this change the dynamics between you?

How might this benefit you?

Stay On-Track with this Trio of Truths

In this part of the book, I talked about the "trio of truths." Write down your thoughts about each of those.

Part Three:

His "Friendships" With Other Women and Extramarital Affairs

And Up We Go

Here in part three of the book, I'm going to be focusing on those situations where a husband's midlife crisis has escalated to the point of infidelity—where he is striking up very close friendships with other women, and where there is an element of betrayal involved. That may be an emotional affair or a full-blown physical affair where he's moving out of the home and moving in with his girlfriend.

To be clear, this part of the book deals with spouses who are behaving about as badly as they can, so I'll be speaking very plainly and very openly about that. This can be very ugly behavior and it can take a serious toll a wife's well-being.

As always, I am in no way suggesting that all men do this. Of course they don't. Frankly, the vast majority of men would never do this to themselves or to their wives.

But some do. When a man's midlife episode becomes very self-focused and self-indulgent, when his ego or drive for reinvention takes over—and it can, even temporarily, even without any kind of sinister aspect to it—it is possible that he will try to validate his self-image by getting attention from another, possibly younger, woman.

And that can take a toll on his wife's self-esteem, her dignity, her power and her clear thinking. She has no idea how to respond to it. In her confusion, worry and sadness, she can lose sight of herself and of the situation as it really is. She's too close, too emotional, to see it clearly or objectively.

That's why I speak very plainly in this part of the book. If you're a wife whose husband is behaving this poorly, who is betraying your trust and love, you need clarity. You also need a bit of an attitude! You need to regain your dignity, your power, and your objectivity.

The Midlife Man & Other (Younger) Women

We can all picture the stereotype of the midlife man, cruising around town with a much younger woman in the passenger seat of his convertible. Some people might laugh when they think of this. They see it as amusing, maybe a little sad: an aging man trying to recapture his fading youth by hooking up with a younger woman. It doesn't make him look more virile, it just emphasizes his age and insecurities.

At the same time, people aren't generally impressed by his younger girlfriend. There is an assumption that she has ulterior motives for hooking up with a man who's old enough to be her father, and those reasons have less to do with a burning desire for his body, and more to do with a burning desire for his bank account.

But a person who is in the throes of a self-focused midlife crisis doesn't always see things critically or objectively. Sometimes their egos won't let them. Sometimes they just don't want to admit it to themselves. The truth is far less pleasant than the fantasy.

I remember a case where the husband was fifty-five and his girlfriend was twenty-eight. He was a wealthy businessman, and she was a struggling single mom with two young kids. So it was perhaps natural that she saw financial security when she looked at him. They met at some kind of mixer for his company—she was a waitress—and soon thereafter started having an affair.

Eventually, his wife investigated the unusual charges on their credit card—clothes and gifts for his girlfriend, and for her children—and discovered the affair. When she confronted him, he didn't deny it, didn't apologize.

Instead, he said something very close to this, *"I'm a very sexual man and I have needs...and she's younger, so she has the energy to fulfill those needs."*

Now of course, this wife initially reacted instinc emotionally. She lost it, and said, *"Are you kidding ¡ starving waitress gives you a blowjob in a hotel room and you .... you're all that? She's playing you for an old fool. Don't you know that people are laughing at you behind your back?"*

It's too bad this wife didn't consult me before confronting her husband and launching into it like this. Because I could've told her how it was going to go down.

Her husband did not see the light. He did not agree with her or consider the possibility that this younger, financially struggling woman might be using him for his money (and honestly, we can understand that—sometimes it's about surviving). Instead, this man dug in his heels to prove that his wife was wrong and that he was, in fact, quite the stud.

He told his wife that he had finally found someone he was more compatible with physically and sexually. And the more he spewed this kind of thing, the more he actually started to believe it.

That's why throughout this book I've warned you against getting into those pointless arguments. I've warned you against challenging him outright or telling him how foolish he looks or is acting. When you do this, you only trigger a defensive response. And the more he defends himself, the more he may begin to believe what he's saying, and his egotistical way of thinking may grow.

The funny thing about people with inflated egos (temporarily or not) is that their behavior is often a mask for insecurity. It's smoke and mirrors. Inside, they feel vulnerable. They need the validation of others, that's why they present themselves to others as a really awesome person.

When you challenge that, they will react to protect the way they want to see themselves. That is true of all people who want to believe something about themselves, not just those in the throes of a midlife episode.

You are hurt, and I understand how much you want to tell him that he's not nearly as amazing, or attractive or energetic or unique or virile as he thinks he is. But remember what you've learned to this point. Don't get into a pointless argument.

* * * * * * *

FROM DON'S DESK

I mentioned this is part two, but I have to remind you here—if you insult his manhood or virility (which is understandably very tempting to do if he's with another woman), I guarantee he will remember those words for a long time. They might ring in his ears so loud and for long that, even if he wants to reconcile with you in the future, the memory of those words will stop him. If he feels that you don't see him as a man, he may think there is no point returning to you. It's just too hard on his ego and sense of self. There are other ways to assert yourself and step back from him. Use those instead of insults, especially if you really do hope he will snap out of it at some point and be honestly willing to recommit to you.

* * * * * * *

At the same time, you do also have to accept the sometimes hurtful truth that your husband, despite his age, may still feel attracted to other or younger women. Most men are. In the same way, a lot of mature women are still attracted to other men, sometimes younger, sometimes not.

The difference is that most people have the humility, maturity and perspective to know that it's one thing to have the odd fantasy and another thing to blow your life apart so you can pursue it as a reality. A man who is going through a serious midlife crisis loses those things.

On top of that, our society tells men, even older and (to put it bluntly) unattractive men that they are desirable to younger women. That's why most advertising and movies and so on feature an older man paired with a younger woman. It's a message advertisers rely on to sell to men, and if your husband is going through a serious midlife episode, he's going to buy it.

A lot of wives will say that their midlife husband will more and more begin to check out younger women. Whether they're out for dinner or walking through the mall, they'll see his eyes start to wander. They may start to gravitate toward being around younger women and they may even start to compare their wife to these younger women.

They may say things like, *"You should wear a dress like that,"* or *"do you remember when you looked like that or had that kind of energy?"*

You must always remember that when he acts like this, he only projecting onto you his own feelings of insecurity and his own issues with aging.

It is not about you. It's about him.

But it still hurts, doesn't it?

If you see this starting to happen, or if it's already happening, don't react. Rather, just tell him (once!) that it hurts your feelings. If he apologizes and stops doing it, great.

But he might not apologize or stop doing it.

He might just deny he's doing it, or he might qualify his behavior by saying something like, *"I wasn't being mean, I was just making an observation. It's not my fault if you're insecure or oversensitive. It's natural for me to look. Maybe if you felt better about yourself you wouldn't be so hurt."*

So basically, he may find a way to absolve himself of guilt and turn it around so you're the one who's acting unreasonably.

The Shut-Out Wife

If he does this, don't engage. Just shrug it off. It's pointless to argue. Moreover, don't say it again. That just lets him know that he can keep doing it and get away with it—you might complain, but you're not actually going to do anything about it. Instead, let your actions speak for you.

Let's say you're out for dinner and he starts staring at the waitress—not just a passing glance at a pretty girl, but staring or engaging with her to the point that it's disrespectful to you. Undressing her with his eyes, so to speak.

If that happens, simply ask for the bill and leave. If he gets angry or says you're overreacting or too sensitive or whatever, simply shrug it off. Don't argue. You can respond by saying something like, *"Well, we all have our own way of seeing things."*

Don't challenge his behavior. Why not? Because—as I've said before—he knows what he's doing. But he's either so self-absorbed or so indifferent to you that he's doing it anyway...either way, it's unlikely that challenging him will get you anywhere. It's more likely that he'll find a way to make it about you. It's more likely that the two of you will still end up arguing, although just for a different reason. At least this way, you are respecting yourself.

In fact, the more your husband disrespects you, the more self-respect you will need. That's how you're going to protect yourself.

Your best and maybe only option is to let you behavior speak for you. Let him see, through your actions, that you're simply not going to remain in a situation where he or anyone else is going to make you feel uncomfortable or bad about yourself. You don't have to stand up and throw a glass of water in his face or make a scene or storm off like a drama queen. Always conduct yourself like the graceful, self-respecting woman you are! Stay in control of your own emotions, thoughts and responses.

But as always, you need to be prepared for his reaction. Because when you don't react, he will.

The Shut-Out Wife

When you respond with dignity and with self-control, you basically take back your power. That's what personal empowerment is. It's the confidence and ability to respond and act in the ways that you know are best for you.

If your husband is becoming self-indulgent and self-focused, he won't want you to do that. Yes, he might get mad if you leave a restaurant early, but aren't you mad that he's staring at the waitress's ass? To be honest, the waitress is probably mad about it, too. I often tell my clients that "mad doesn't matter." We all get mad, every day, over all kinds of things. But if someone is behaving rudely toward you, you don't have to just sit there and allow it to happen.

You're a grown woman. You have the liberty to do as you like. It doesn't matter if your partner gets mad. You aren't to blame for that. He might only be mad because he can't keep doing what he's doing. Whatever he's been doing has been working for him, and when you refuse to indulge that, he gets mad. We all get mad when someone makes us stop doing something we want to do, or when they make that difficult for us.

Now, of course you always need to self-check your own behavior to make sure you aren't over-reacting or that you aren't part of the problem. That's the kind of thing I talked about extensively in part one. But in this part, we're dealing with situations where you've done everything you can on your end, and where you're confident it's your husband who is choosing to openly disrespect you and your marriage.

I'm also assuming that you're not concerned about any safety issues when you begin to empower yourself like this. If you are, you shouldn't be reading this or any book. Rather, you should be reaching out for help from an appropriate resource (a mental health professional, a lawyer, even the police). As always, you know your husband and situation best. If you're concerned about asserting yourself in a reasonable and respectful way, then you need help and advice that goes beyond the scope of this book.

But barring that, remember—mad doesn't matter. When it comes down it, a midlife spouse's behavior can sometimes be so obnoxious and self-focused that there's simply no way to avoid some kind of strain or conflict. There's no way to avoid them getting mad or being unhappy at the way you respond, or choose not to engage.

Since that's the case, you might as well choose to respond in a way that allows you to keep your dignity and to show him, through your actions, that you're simply not going to remain in the presence of someone who is disrespecting you. Shrug it off and walk away.

What to Do When He Strikes Up a Close "Friendship" with Another Woman

I want to turn now to a situation that often develops—when a man in the throes of a midlife episode begins to strike up friendships with other women.

In part two, when I was going through the six parts of a midlife episode, I said that men often befriend younger women who are divorced or who are single mothers. In many cases it's a symbiotic relationship. He's looking for the validation of a younger woman, and she's looking for the resources of an older man. But as you've learned, what may be obvious to most people will not be obvious to him. Mark Twain famously said that it's easier to fool a person than it is to convince them they've been fooled.

Men in midlife may also strike up friendships with other women, younger or not, who are married but who say they are in unhappy marriages. They often meet these women at work or at some kind of fitness or hobby activity.

Whether or not the woman's marriage is truly unhappy or not remains to be seen. Some women simply enjoy the attention of another man, so they start to play the damsel in distress. *"Oh, my husband is so mean to me."*

The Shut-Out Wife

This can make an older man feel like her rescuer or her confidant, almost like he has to protect her from her mean husband. It's often an act, but it's one that men do fall for.

It is less common for single, never married and child-free women to hook up with older married men. Those women—at least those with options—aren't typically interested in someone else's middle-aged husband, and all the drama and baggage that goes with that. They just aren't into the whole mistress thing.

Yet a younger woman might want to hook up with an older man for a reason you might not immediately think of, and that's because the relationship makes her feel as good about herself as it makes him feel about himself. He wants to feel adored and desired by a younger woman, and she gives him that ego boost; however, she also wants to feel admired and that she's special. An older man might make her feel this way, while men her own age probably aren't as dazzled by her. So it's an ego-boost and a validation for both of them, although for different reasons. Some women who grew up without fathers may also be drawn to older men. They're looking for a husband and father in one.

Why am I telling you all of this? After all, you probably already know some of it, and you've heard it before. But it is worth repeating for an extremely important reason.

Wives often see their husband's new female friend, whether she becomes an affair partner or not, as something of a mystery woman. You might assume that she's the perfect woman or that she has some kind of magical or irresistible appeal that you don't.

You might assume that she's the total package—a barely-legal gymnast who gets straight A's in medical school and who makes extra money by being a lingerie model. You might assume this woman is amazing and so much more together and beautiful and interesting than you are.

If that's what you're thinking or assuming, you may need to see her and the situation a lot more clearly and objectively. It isn't about her. She could be anyone.

It's about your husband's perception of himself, and his attempts to validate the new him. It's about how she makes him feel about himself. If she were a real catch, she wouldn't be playing third-wheel in someone else's midlife marriage.

But people are people, and we assume the worst. If your husband strikes up a friendship with another woman, younger or not, of course you're going to worry that she's more beautiful, sexy, and interesting than you are. Of course you're going to worry that he'll find her more desirable and that the two of them will end up being happier than you and he ever were.

But statistics don't back that up. Relationships that begin as affairs fail at an overwhelming rate. Most women who get involved with married men, whether it's a midlife crisis situation or not, don't tend to be the cream of the crop.

Many have personal issues and their own demons to contend with. Many are good at attracting men, but once the rush and excitement of the infatuation phase is over, men quickly realize that she isn't *all that* after all. That's how it often plays out.

Moreover, May-December romances (relationships where there is a very significant age gap) also tend to fail. We've all seen ones that work, and they certainly can, but statistically, the odds are against it. What often happens in these situations is that a parent-child dynamic develops, or the couple simply finds they're at different stages of their lives. Again, it might work for a while, but like so many things when it comes to relationships, the fantasy eventually wears thin and reality kicks in.

I guess I'm also telling you this because I want you to have a bit of a chip on your shoulder—not in a bitchy or belligerent way, but just in a quietly confident way. I want you to see his relationships with other women as they likely are, and I want you to see those other women as they likely are...they're probably not nearly as amazing as you assume or fear that they are.

That kind of thinking, that kind of chip on your shoulder, can give you clarity and perspective. It's a layer of self-protection.

Naturally, it's a frightening and hurtful thing to know that your husband is befriending other women, especially when he's already behaving in such uncharacteristic or untrustworthy ways. That's why you need think long-term and you need to stay in control of your own emotions and responses.

If he starts to hang around more women or strikes up a friendship with one woman in particular, you can tell him that it makes you uncomfortable. If he cares, he'll stop doing it. But chances are, he'll find a way to keep doing it, while also finding a way to turn it around so that you come across as an insecure or controlling wife.

Please, think twice about falling into that dynamic where you repeatedly try to explain why you're hurt or why what he's doing is inappropriate, and where he denies it or turns it back onto you.

If he knows you're hurt or uncomfortable and he's still doing it, it's pointless to keep repeating yourself. It only makes you look weak and desperate. It only reinforces his perception that he is the one who holds all the power. On top of that, it might go to his head—the fact that he has a female friend and you're clearly jealous may only feed his ego all the more.

Also, resist the urge to speak disparagingly about this other woman. It's pointless to try to convince him that she's out for his money, or that she's some kind of messed up basket case. You'll only look petty and jealous.

A man who is going through a midlife episode and who strikes up a friendship with another woman will often cling very tightly to that friendship. He will be protective of it. And if he feels you are threatening that friendship or slandering his friend, he may begin to see you as the enemy as he defends this other woman's presence in his life.

Finally, do not—I repeat, do not!—reach out to this other woman. Don't call or text her, don't message her on social media. Again, you'll only look petty and jealous. You'll also look like you have no control over your own emotions or behavior.

ad, she'll clue in really quickly that you have no control
arriage or husband, either. If you did, you wouldn't be
So don't give her that kind of importance.

So, all of this begs the question: what do you actually do if your husband strikes up a close friendship with another woman? I've told you what not to do, but are there proactive steps you can take to end this friendship?

Yes. You can begin by focusing on what I've said here—on how this fantasy woman of his isn't as fantastic as he might think. He might not know it yet, but you probably do. Remind yourself that she isn't special. It isn't about her. She could be any woman that he met and that fulfilled his current needs or self-perception.

Rather, it's about him and the narrative he wants to create. It's about him, and the ego boost or erotic thrill that he wants to experience.

Depersonalize her. When you think of her, don't picture her face, don't even think her name. Imagine her as a faceless, nameless person. Strip her of her identity and importance in your own mind. That will help prevent you from feeling that you have to compare yourself to her or compete with her.

If you feel the friendship is truly inappropriate, and especially if you feel it has become or is on the verge of becoming an emotional affair, by all means say that to your husband. State your truth clearly: *"I feel this friendship is taking a toll on our marriage."*

If you feel it's in the best interests of your marriage, you can also ask him to end it. I suggest saying something like this:

"I know you enjoy so-and-so's friendship, but for the good of our marriage I'm asking you to stop seeing her so that we can focus on us. You might be losing a good friend, but you'd be gaining a happy wife who would really love to make you happy again."

If he ends the friendship, great.

But if doesn't, do not ask again.

You heard me, right? Do not ask again.

He knows you don't like it. He knows you want it to end. Instead, you may want to proceed as if the friendship is an emotional affair, providing that you truly feel it is one. You don't need his permission or agreement to do that. You do need to trust your own assessment of the situation.

As someone who has specialized in infidelity issues for a long time, I often advise people to make a real change when they put that "emotional affair" label on the friendship their spouse is having with another person.

This might involve withdrawing emotional intimacy. After all, he's already been doing that to you. It does you no good to keep offering him emotional support or comfort if he currently prefers to get that from another person. That only sets you up for rejection. It also shows him that you're willing to live with the situation, and that you're willing to undermine the exclusive emotional connection that should exist between a husband and wife, by letting this other woman be part of it. So unless you're into threesomes, you might not want to do this.

You might also want to move into separate bedrooms in the home and refrain from sexual intimacy. These are scary thoughts, I know. You might worry that if you pull away like this, he will just sort of drift away and that his relationship with her will get even closer. And that's possible. That's why, in the end, you need to put a lot of thought into the strategies I offer in this book, and decide which ones you feel are right for you. My job is to present you with some new ideas and insights so that you aren't just spinning your wheels. My job is also to tell you what I've seen work for other women in your situation. Your job is to decide what to do with that.

So here's my take. If he's drifting away anyway, if he's growing ever-closer to another woman anyway, where is the benefit in passively allowing that to happen under your nose without taking any steps to say, "*Hey, I'm not living like this…I'm not going to pretend it isn't happening. I am going to respond.*"

To me, this may be a better approach than simply doing nothing as his friendship with another woman continues to deepen to the point that it's a betrayal of the intimacy in your marriage.

If you take no action, at least no action other than complaining or crying, you basically show him that he can get away with it. There are no consequences. And when there are no consequences, people tend to do as they like. So I don't think that putting your head in the sand and quietly waiting it out presents you as a truly empowered person.

Now, will he get mad that he has to sleep in the guest room or that you decide to move into it? Will he find a way to turn it around and blame it on you, or say that you're too sensitive or overreacting, or whatever? Might he try to say that you're the one who's giving up on the marriage? Maybe. Probably.

Remember, whenever you take your personal power back, whenever you empower yourself and exercise some kind of control, he will likely react to that. As I've said, a midlife man's behavior can sometimes be so self-indulgent and self-focused that there's simply no way to avoid some kind conflict. So if that's the case, you might as well respond in a way that allows you to keep your dignity and to show him, through your actions, that you're simply not going to remain in the presence of someone who is disrespecting you.

How to Know If He's Having an Affair

Picture this: I'm walking down the street with my sister when I point to a little fluffy brown animal behind a fence. It's wearing a red collar with a tag that says *Fido*, it's barking and it's wagging its tail. What is it? That's right, it's a dog. If I say to my sister, "*Hey, that's a dog*," she's going to nod and say, "*Yes, Deb, that's a dog.*" Not much room for debate there.

The Shut-Out Wife

Now picture this. I'm sitting in my office with a couple. The wife says, "*I found the text messages that he sent her...he said she was beautiful, he called her 'sunshine' and said he couldn't wait to see her again.*"

The husband speaks up. "*It was just a few stupid text messages. It's not like I was cheating on you.*"

So let me ask you. What is it? Is it infidelity? Is it cheating? Or is just a few meaningless text messages?

You'd be surprised how often couples argue about this very thing—about the definition of infidelity, about what is cheating and what isn't.

Here, the wife might say, "*I know you're having an affair.*"

The husband will likely respond by saying, "*No, I'm not.*"

My point is this: do not exhaust yourself trying to "prove" to him, or to yourself for that matter, that he's having an affair. You're not in a courtroom. It isn't about evidence, it's about the quality of your intimacy as a couple.

It's about the level of trust you're feeling toward your husband. If trust is lacking, there's a problem. And if the trust you have in him is waning, then your trust in yourself must absolutely rise to compensate for that.

You must learn to trust and to reply upon your own assessment of what's happening.

You know your husband and your marriage better than anyone else. Learning to trust your own gut, to rely upon your own assessment of the situation, can save you all kinds of frustration. It can help you avoid a ton of pointless arguments where you say "*You're cheating*" and he says "*No, I'm not.*"

You know him. Trust that knowledge. Be fair, be open-minded. But in the end, we all have to draw our own conclusions. Nowhere is that more true than when it comes to unfaithfulness in marriage.

That's because, in many cases, the other spouse is doing everything they can be deceptive, to downplay the situation, to defect the blame or conversation somewhere else, or to debate the issue, trying to muddy the waters so their partner doesn't see the situation clearly.

That being said, there are some common signs that suggest a person is having an affair.

One of the first is secrecy, especially with respect to his phone, computer, and online accounts. He'll guard his phone and carry it with him everywhere. He'll change the password and refuse to share it with you. He'll delete his text and call history. He'll get defensive or angry if you ask to look at his phone.

His behavior toward you will probably change in some way. He'll either be super sweet to compensate for what he's doing and basically distract you from it, or he'll be more critical and distant. He'll either be more sexual with you or less sexual. It's the change in his behavior that gives him away.

He'll also start taking better care of himself. He'll embark on a fitness regime and start dressing better, maybe even trying out different styles of clothing or different colognes.

You'll also notice a change in his routine and schedule. He'll just sort of disappear off the radar for a while as he spends time with the other woman...so he'll either say he's doing something else, maybe working or exercising, or he'll just go MIA and won't tell you where he's been.

When you ask him about his behavior or whereabouts, he will probably react defensively. He'll try to turn it around so that you feel pretty small or petty about questioning him. After all, nobody wants to be "that wife" who's always checking up on her husband. It's demeaning, and so one way he gets you to back off is by making you feel that way.

He may also dismiss your feelings—sadness, worry, betrayal—and instead insist that you provide facts to back up your "accusations." This is where that debate element can come in.

Let's say you found a text he sent to another woman...one where he called her "beautiful."

You might say, *"It's hurtful and inappropriate for you to say something like that to another woman. Don't you understand that?"*

In response, he will say, *"I was just commenting on her appearance. Tell me how that's cheating?"*

You see this tactic, right? Instead of addressing your feelings or his behavior, he's turned the spotlight onto you. Now all of a sudden you're sputtering for words, trying to explain to him why what he's doing is wrong and why you're hurt by it.

And the more you do this, the more you're baffled....why doesn't he get it? Why doesn't he understand what I'm saying? So you find about a gazillion different ways to say it, although none of them seem to sink in with him.

Except that, in reality, he does know what he's doing and he does know what you're saying. He gets it! Either he's going to show concern and respect for your feelings, or he isn't. Either he's going to be honest and collaborative or he isn't. And if he isn't, you will find yourself spinning your wheels in that baffling, frustrating place of repeatedly trying to get through to him.

But until he's ready to listen and reconnect with you, it won't happen. That's why you must learn to trust and rely upon your own assessment of the situation. If your gut is telling you that he has somehow strayed from the fidelity and privacy of your marriage, if your gut is telling you that his behavior is untrustworthy, then you may be right.

And if that's the case, it will likely be a futile endeavor to try and extract some kind of admission from him. Instead, you're likely better off learning to trust your own assessment of what is happening. Do not engage in endless debate about it. Do not repeatedly defend yourself or explain yourself. Not only will this keep you mired in anxiety, it will result in all kinds of pointless arguments between the two of you.

Might there come a time when he is willing to open up and work with you to save your marriage? I hope so. But if he's shut you out right now, you simply can't force your way back in. The damage you'll do trying to break through the wall he's put up just isn't worth it.

When He Wants to Move Out and Get His Own Place

As a man's midlife episode continues to escalate, the time may come when he shatters his wife's world by saying these words: *"I want to move out...I want to get my own place."*

If his behavior hasn't yet thrown his wife into panic mode, this will probably do it. And typically, a wife will react out of fear and emotion. She will start to ask him why he wants to move out, does that mean he wants a divorce, how long will he move out for, doesn't he love her any more...and so on.

Unfortunately, she probably won't get any kind of meaningful answers from him. He will have no words of comfort or clarity to reassure her.

Instead, her head will spin with those unanswered questions. *Is my marriage over? Is he leaving me? Has he lost all love for me? Is he having an affair?*

If you're in this situation, or if you come to find yourself in this situation, you will probably react by trying to get your husband to remain in your home and not move out.

You may cry or beg him not to go. This probably won't work. And even if did work, he would be so distant and bitter about it that it would only harm your marriage anyway. It would be counterproductive in the extreme.

A man in the throes of a midlife episode is usually only (or at least primarily) thinking of himself. He prioritizes his own preferences and importance. Therefore, when you beg him to stay, you reinforce that sense of priority and self-importance.

That's why I advise women to respond and not just react, and especially to respond in a way that may be unfamiliar to him. Later, you will learn about a concept that I often talk about in my practice and books, and that's the idea of defamiliarization. For our purposes, this means presenting something very familiar (whether a person, a behavior or some other thing) in a way that is unfamiliar and unusual, thus provoking a more impactful response. It can be a creative and effective strategy in terms of communication and conflict resolution, but it can be effective in this capacity, too.

Consider this. Instead of crying and begging him to stay, instead of asking him a barrage of questions that he probably won't answer, simply pause and say nothing when he says he wants to move out. Resist that sense of urgency that's rising up in you, urging you to question him or cry or plead with him to stay. Just slow that whole process down. Let him see, with his own eyes, that you aren't going to collapse into a heap of raw emotion. Let him see that you're thinking about it. That you're mulling it over. That may surprise him, since he may be expecting an instant reaction.

Then, instead of begging him to stay or questioning him (especially if you've already been doing this and it's become a familiar reaction), you may want to respond by saying something along the lines of, *"That might be a good idea for both of us."*

In all probability, he will not be expecting this measured response. And he will certainly not be expecting to hear that you might actually be okay with his moving out or that you might actually want him to go for your own reasons.

Therefore, your response can give him a dose of perspective: *"Hey, I might not actually be calling all the shots here."*

Your response can also be a bit of a shocker: *"Why isn't she asking me to stay? What is she thinking?"*

One of my ongoing goals in this book is to return your marriage to a state where both the motivation to save the marriage, and the balance of power within it, is shared equally and healthily between you and your husband.

Instead of you constantly analyzing him and wondering what he's thinking or going to do, instead of him calling all the shots, we level that out. We create a dynamic where he starts to wonder what you're thinking, too. He needs to realize that you are just as empowered as he is, and that you have just as much control over this marriage as he does. You are just as capable of self-determination as he is. The sooner you can send that message, the better.

Yet as with so many things in this book, this is easier said than done. It's hard to act like you're okay with his moving out when it scares you so much. It's hard to act like you think it might be a good idea when in reality you think it's the worst idea ever.

But let me challenge that. If he does want to move out, you know as well as I do that there's no stopping him. He's an adult, he can go if he wants. Every day that you guilt or pressure him into staying is one more day where his irritation and resentment of you grows. Think about it. If you don't want to be around someone but they basically force you to stay, your feelings for them don't get better, do they? Of course not. Your feelings only deteriorate.

Every time he passes you in the hall, every time he sees you in the living room watching television, every time he hears you on the phone talking to someone, he gets a little more irritated by you. If he doesn't want to be there, if he doesn't truly want to be around you, that's the risk you take by convincing him to stay.

That's why his moving out may in fact be better for your marriage in the long run. If your continued presence is chipping away at the love he feels for you, if it's reinforcing his increasingly negative perception of you, then your best bet may be to put some distance between you. It's like that old saying—absence makes the heart grow fonder. We don't have a chance to miss someone or think about them if they're always there with us.

Plus, I want you think what his moving out might mean for you on a day to day basis. No more watching him mope around the house. No more walking on eggshells around him. No more living your life around what might make him happy or set him off.

No more living with the heartache of having him so close, yet so far away. No more having to live with his mixed messages or comments or mood swings.

His moving out might be a liberating thing for you. It might give you some perspective and room to catch your breath. You might enjoy living a home that is free of anxiety and tension.

So just give all of this a think.

Think about responding instead of reacting, and especially think about responding in a way that will surprise him: *"That might be a good idea for both of us."* Do the unexpected. Don't ask a bunch of questions, don't beg him to stay.

Another important thing to point out here. If he says he wants to move out, don't keep asking him about it. Don't follow up with him by asking whether he's been looking for a place. Many wives do this, hoping he'll turn around and say, *"No, I've changed my mind. I'm staying home."*

But as you know, a man who is going through a destructive midlife episode is not going to be a source of reassurance for you. Stop trying to get it from him. It only drives him further away and causes you anxiety and frustration.

It's common for a midlife man to say he's going to move out or that he wants to, but then do nothing about it. Men like this are often impulsive and driven by their changing emotions. One minute he wants to go, the next he doesn't. And they'll often say whatever is on their mind: *"I want to move out,"* and a short time later, *"No, I'm going to stay."* They change with the wind. That's why you need to step back, out of the storm, and disengage. Stop living in his wake and reacting to everything he says and does.

Now, let's say he does move out. Here's what **not** to do. Do not ask him about his new place. Do not ask him what it's like or how long it takes him to get to work. Do not ask him if it has good laundry facilities. Do not contact him. Do not call him, text him or email him anything of a personal nature. If you need to send something business related, do so, but do not include a personal note.

.   Do not remind him that his sister's birthday is on Friday or your son's karate tournament is on the weekend. Remember back in part two when I told you that you're not his counselor? Well, you're not his secretary, either. Some wives tend to "mother" their husbands when they move out. They'll ask if they need help with anything, or if they have everything they need. They'll try to make themselves useful to him, hoping that he'll realize how much he needs her and what a fool he is for leaving. Please, do not do this. It's desperate, it's degrading, and it will backfire.

Similarly, do not tell him that you miss him and do not ask him to come home. Do not invite him for supper. If a pipe under the sink springs a leak, do not call him to come and fix it. Call a plumber. Accept the fact that you are living alone. Act like it.

All right—these are some ideas of how you might handle yourself and the situation if he says he wants to move out. But *why* does he want to move out? No doubt that's a question you want answered.

It may be that he really does just need some space to think about his life. Or he may want to recapture a feeling of youthful freedom and independence and to do that he needs to get away from his responsibilities and obligations at home. It may be that he wants to come and go as he likes, without having to answer to you.

Or, and this is something you need to know, he may be having an affair, preparing to have an affair, or even just thinking about it. It isn't unusual for unfaithful spouses to move out and get their own place, and this can be for obvious reasons.

Now, some practitioners will encourage you to set boundaries if your husband moves out. They'll advise you to tell him—in no uncertain terms—that even though you're living apart, you're still legally married and that means you aren't free to have sex with other people.

By now you might be able to predict my take on this. He knows you're legally married. He knows that extramarital relations are not going to be acceptable. So I ask you—why waste your breath saying this? It doesn't matter if you get a vow of fidelity from him. It doesn't matter if he agrees to abide by your boundaries. If he wants to be with someone else, he will do it regardless of what he says or promises, and regardless of your boundaries. That's why I urge you to take what he says (good or bad) with a grain of salt.

Keep your emotions in check. Respond, do not react. Steer clear of long conversations or explanations. Don't bother threatening him or setting boundaries that he already knows exist. Accept the fact that you now live alone. As a general rule, shrug off what he says or does, and walk away. If he wants you, he'll catch up to you.

When He's Unfaithful

It's one of the most shocking and heartbreaking experiences a woman can face—finding out that her husband has been unfaithful. It's a devastating experience no matter how old you are. A young woman with small children at home faces the prospect of breaking up her family and being a single mom. A middle-aged or more mature woman faces the prospect of living her retirement years as a single woman.

But let's face it. We've all known women who have found themselves in this situation, and who, as horrible as the situation can be, have come out the other side stronger and happier than ever. That's important to remember. Because finding out your husband has cheated can be an all-consuming experience. It can make you lose perspective in your life. It can make you feel like the other parts of your life don't have value or have lost their significance.

And forgive me, but that's bullshit. So I'll do my best to help you get through this, and even to help you put your marriage back together if that's what you want. There are definitely behaviors on your part that can give you a better chance of making that happen, and I'll talk about those.

But your attitude is key. You have to find a way to keep perspective in your life and to find comfort and meaning beyond your marriage. You have to have dignity and know that life will go on, a good life will go on, even without him. Because when you have that kind of perspective, you have power. And at this time in your life, you are going to need to feel as empowered as possible.

Self-care is also essential during this time. You absolutely must take care of yourself emotionally, mentally, physically and spiritually. Reach out to the right people, whether that's your doctor or counselor, a spiritual advisor or a good friend. Get the help you need to get through the day and to sleep through the night. And then combine the strength you receive from those resources with the strategies I offer in this book—pick and choose the ones you think have the best chance of working. All of this is part and parcel of empowering and equipping you with what you need to get through this and to act in ways that are in your best interests.

Let's move on to the nuts and bolts. A woman might discover that her husband is having an affair in any number of ways, but nowadays, she often finds out via technology. She might come across a text message, a telling social media post, or a wayward email.

She might also be alerted by a change in his behavior. He may be more loving and attentive than usual. More likely, though, his behavior is cold. He may begin or increase his efforts to re-write his marital history, blame his wife for any marriage problems, or find some other way to regard her in a more negative light so he can justify, even to himself, what he is doing.

In any event, his wife discovers his infidelity.

At this point, she will probably want to know certain facts. Who is this other person? Are they in love or is it just physical? Where did they meet? When did it start and how long has it been going on? Is it still going on? How did or do they communicate or see each other?

Sometimes, an unfaithful partner is remorseful and motivated to save their marriage, so they'll answer these kinds of questions. They may not admit to everything with total honesty, at least not right away, but they will answer questions. They know they have to if they want to hold onto their marriage.

Unfortunately, that's not typically the case with affairs that happen during midlife episodes. In these situations, a man is usually in the full throes of that self-indulgent state. He's re-written his history with his wife and he doesn't always feel motivated to save the marriage, at least not at that point in time. That motivation may come down the road as the fantasy wears off and reality kicks in, but that may take a while.

So where does that leave you if you've discovered he's been unfaithful? Well, I've already give you some initial suggestions of what to do. Strive for that perspective so that you can keep your power. Care for yourself emotionally, mentally, physically and spiritually. I'd also recommend that you protect yourself financially, particularly if the affair is ongoing and he will not end it. If that means booking an appointment with a lawyer for advice, so be it.

But back to those facts and questions about the infidelity. Who is this other person, does he love her (or does he think he loves her), is it emotional or physical or both, where did they meet, when did it start, is it still going on? How did or do they talk or meet up? These are questions that of course you want answered.

You may already know some of the answers. You may know the identity of the other woman and where they met and so on.

As for the things you don't know, you can certainly ask him. You have every right to ask. Will he answer, or answer honestly? Who knows.

But whether he answers or not, will it change anything? Probably not. That's especially true if the affair is still going on. You can ask him to end it, but whether he will is another matter.

Unless and until he wants to return to your marriage, unless and until he is remorseful and willing to be honest, unless and until he is the one who is actively working to save your marriage, it may be pointless to ask these questions. It may be pointless to ask him to end the affair. He knows it's wrong to have an affair while you're married. If he were willing to end it, he would do so on his own.

I'm going to let you in on a little professional secret. I've worked for years with couples who are struggling with infidelity, and in most cases, it's the betrayed spouse who reaches out to me first. They are the one booking appointments, or doing research on infidelity, or trying to convince their partner to stay with them.

But it has to be the other way around. It has to be the unfaithful partner who willingly ends the affair and works their way back into the marriage. It has to be the unfaithful partner who begs for their spouse's forgiveness, who is honest, who is accountable, and who is empathetic to what they've put their spouse through.

It has to be the unfaithful partner who leads the way. They know what they've done. And the more you wag your finger at them, the more you try to extract information from them or tell them how they've hurt you or why they'll regret what they done, the less motivated they are to save the marriage or repair the damage they've done. Why? Because the more you do, the less they have to do. The more you ask questions and ask them to stay, the more they realize they're in relative control of the situation.

Know this: If he's shut you out of his life by having an affair, he is the one who must open the door and ask you to come back in.

So…where does all of this leave you right now? It leaves you with a very personal decision to make. Is infidelity a deal-breaker for you? Is it something you feel you could move past? Is divorce the only option you're willing to look at? Only you can answer that.

Some women will end their marriage after an infidelity. They just know they couldn't get past it, and they don't want to put themselves through the emotional turmoil of trying. To them, the marriage and the partnership has just changed too much.

And that's something to think about. I have seen situations where a woman wanted nothing more than to win her husband back after an infidelity. Yet once she did, and once her emotions and the dust settled, she was left with a different marriage and a lot of things to work through on a personal level.

That's something to consider. Because if your husband does turn around and you do save your marriage, his infidelity will become a part of your story as a couple. It will become a part of your history, and it will affect your intimacy and your trust in him, at least for some time.

I'm not saying it can't be overcome, because it can. If both of you really want to get past it and really try, it can be done. But it takes a lot of time, work and soul-searching.

To be clear, this is not me dissuading you from trying to save your marriage. Not at all. It's your decision. I'm only encouraging you to look at things from all angles, and to think of your own needs and your own best interests, both now and into the future.

Now, let's say you've done a lot of thinking, and you've decided that you aren't willing to end your marriage, or that you need more time to see what your husband will do, or to see how you feel about things. That's great. That's what this book is here for.

I know you don't want to give up on your marriage too easily, and I know you don't want to have any second thoughts, doubts or regrets.

So as you go through this part of the book, I'll continue to help you figure out what behaviors on your part are most likely, and least likely, to get you what you do want.

When He Won't End His Affair

I'd like to say that most men who are unfaithful during a midlife episode immediately respond to what they've done with remorse and honesty. I would like to say that they immediately end the affair, apologize to their wife and start the process of rebuilding the marriage and reconnecting as a couple.

But I can't say that. Because in my professional experience, most men who are having a destructive midlife crisis and who are unfaithful will not feel remorse or apologize, at least not right away. As far as they're concerned, they're entitled to that kind of excitement and pleasure. That is consistent with their self-focus.

Some men also believe they're in love with their affair partner. This is especially true if it's a physical affair with a younger woman. If that's the case, he may cling to the affair quite tightly. Why? Because it makes him feel good. Because it suits the new narrative of his life and his new identity as a youthful, energetic, desirable man. Because it feeds his ego and he feels he deserves it, regardless of the impact it has on the other people in his life.

On top of that, he may be in the early excitement phase of the affair. That's definitely the time when a person (man or woman) of *any* age can be swept up in intense feelings and even mistake those feelings for "love." It wears off, but it can take a while.

If your husband is having an affair and refusing to end it, you can expect him to be protective of this other woman and defensive of the relationship. He may feel that their relationship is special or unique, or that they're destined to be together.

So if you, or a friend or another family member challenges him by saying something like, *"You don't love this person. You barely know her!"* he will likely respond by getting angry and seeing you as the enemy, as someone who is trying to steal his happiness away or who just doesn't understand what he is experiencing.

He may say something like, "*I know how I feel. I know what love is. You have your own reasons for saying that…you don't want me to be happy.*"

* * * * * * *

FROM DON'S DESK

I remember talking to a long-time friend who started an affair with someone he just met and asked me what he should do, since I had some knowledge of his situation.

I said, "Let's look at this logically. You have minor marriage issues that you could probably work through if you put your mind to it. You've been married for ten years and you know your wife is faithful, and a good mom. This woman you're seeing—she's been divorced twice, doesn't have a job, and lives in her parents' basement with her two kids. Do you really think that's going to be a more promising relationship?"

He didn't say anything, so I kept going, assuming he was just taking it all in.

"If you stayed with this other woman, you'd have to get another house where you'd live with her and her kids. Meanwhile, your wife might start dating some other guy, and who knows how he'll treat your kids. And if you end up buying a house with this other woman, it'll be her place, too. Do you know her or trust her enough to take that kind of financial risk with her? Maybe you're better off just trying to work on the relationship you have."

He didn't say anything, just nodded.

I didn't say anything further, either. Not another word. Despite the logic of what I was saying, I could tell that he just didn't care. It wasn't about the logic. It was about what he wanted to do. It really was that simple.

So take it from me. It doesn't matter how much a wife or anyone else tries to reason with a husband who is involved with someone else. If he likes what he's doing, he's going to keep doing it. Logic doesn't matter. The only thing that can influence this is how his wife handles herself, because even if he's involved with someone else, he's still keeping a careful eye on what she is doing.

* * * * * * *

A wife who is faced with this situation—a husband who refuses to end an affair—usually reacts out of emotion. She may plead with him to come back. She may try to persuade him that he's having a midlife crisis and isn't acting rationally.

She may beg him to see a counselor, whether with her or on his own. She may try to explain to him how what he's doing is wrong or how he's hurting her. She may try to warn him about how he's going to regret what he's doing, and how he's destroying not just his long-term marriage, but the relationships he has with other people, including his own children, other family members and friends. She may also ask others to intercede on her behalf.

She may do her best to win him back, trying to prove to him how valuable or playful or sexy she is. She may do everything she can to present herself as a better option than this other woman—so basically, she ends up in a position where she is competing with this other woman.

It is unlikely that any of this will work. It is very possible, in fact, that all of this will have the exact opposite effect. Why? Because when you compete with this other woman, you reinforce the perception that your husband has of himself as this incredibly desirable man—and that's precisely how he wants to feel about himself at this stage of his life. That feeling is at the heart of a midlife crisis.

The last thing you want to do is create a love triangle where two women are basically fighting over him, and he knows it. That can go to anyone's head, never mind someone who is already feeling self-focused or self-indulgent. That person will be in no hurry for the situation to change.

But most of all, when you compete with another woman for your own husband, you forfeit both your dignity and your personal power. You send him the message that he can see another woman and that instead of demanding he stop, instead of protecting yourself by disengaging, you instead actually try to out-do the other woman.

Let me ask you: how will that affect your well-being?

Also, what impression does that give him of you? Like I said—but it is worth repeating—this infidelity will become a part of your history as a couple even if he does come back to you and you decide to work together to save your marriage. Even if you do reconcile, he will always remember your reaction to his affair. If you beg him to end it, if you plead with him to come back, if you compete with another woman for him, he will always remember that. So these may not be wise precedents to set in your marriage or in your life. Think long-term. Will these approaches work in your best interests? I don't think so. But as always, the decision is yours.

The Oldest Relationship Advice in the World

There is one snippet of relationship advice that has been handed down to women throughout the ages, and that piece of advice is so fundamental to female-male dynamics that every matriarch of every tribe and village, every sage woman from prehistory to your red-lipstick-wearing grandmother, has passed it down to other women and girls. Here it is: Don't chase boys!

This golden nugget of advice has been around for so long that I suspect, one day, some archeologist with a grant to study early human dating practices will find it scribbled in an ancient pre-language in some hidden corner of the Lascaux caves.

Don't chase boys. It's deceptively simple, and perhaps to our modern sensibilities, even off-putting. That doesn't mean it doesn't have its applications. It does. There are probably a thousand modern dating methods that use it, even if they've slapped some clever labels on it. That's okay. It was good advice to our club-wielding ancestors, and it's good advice for you, too.

At some point, you'll have to step back and let him come to you. At some point, you may need to test whether triggering that male instinct, that "thrill of the hunt" can work in your situation, albeit in an adapted way.

Let him come to you. Let him pursue you. Let him feel the motivation and thrill of the chase. This is, ultimately, common sense advice. You probably know this is what you need to do. You've probably had friends and family tell you to do this, maybe even beg you to try! That's because it doesn't matter if you're a girl in junior high or a woman in middle age. Boys are boys, and men are men. To be honest, all I'm doing here is reminding you of that ancient wisdom and bringing some structure to how you might want to apply it. Moving forward, that's what we'll spend some time doing.

How to Motivate Him to End His Affair

In the previous section, I talked about what not to do if your husband refuses to end an extramarital affair. I challenged the wisdom of begging him to end it or competing with the other woman.

But are there are actually proactive steps you can take that might motivate him to end the affair?

Yes, there are. Let me ask you—what is motivating him to continue with the affair? The ego boost is certainly part of it. No doubt the novelty and the excitement are, too. So is the forbidden element of it all. In fact, I've found that many unfaithful partners feel drawn to that excitement, that forbidden aspect, as much as or even more than the physical aspect of it.

Let me ask you another question—what makes his relationship with this other woman a forbidden one? I'll tell you. *You* do! The fact that he's with another woman while he's married to you is more than likely contributing to the excitement of the experience. It's more than likely contributing to the ego boost of it all and is prolonging the situation. Two women want him.

It's a pretty logical step from here. If you're the one contributing to the forbidden excitement of it all…well, you need to remove yourself from the equation.

When you step back and refuse to fight for him, when you instead say, *"Hey lady, if you can get him, you can have him,"* you kind of knock the wind out of his sails. You deflate the excitement of it. No longer does he get to indulge in the idea that two woman want him. You're not competing with this other woman—quite the opposite, in fact. Instead, you're basically saying, *"Okay, if you want my cheating midlife husband, he's all yours."*

This may sound harsh; however, this attitude can help you protect yourself, insulate yourself, from your husband's hurtful and disrespectful behavior. It can give a betrayed wife some perspective and help her keep her dignity and her power.

Plus, there have been many times throughout this book when I've encouraged you to resist that initial way of reacting to your husband's behavior and to instead flip the whole thing on its ass, if you'll excuse the vernacular. This is one of those times.

Instead of your husband seeing his mistress as the forbidden one, as the unattainable one that he must pursue or work for, now he sees you—his wife—as the unattainable one, as the one he must catch if he wants to keep her in his life.

This turn of events can take him off guard. One moment he's hunting a rabbit, but then a gazelle suddenly takes off in front of him, and he thinks, *"Hey, maybe that I want that instead."* What self-respecting hunter wouldn't want a gazelle over a rabbit? On top of that, he learns a fast and hard lesson about you, one that makes him think, *"Hey, wait a minute...she isn't desperate for me? She isn't pinning her future on me? She has somewhere else to go?"*

This approach also deflates the excitement that comes from a forbidden or secret affair. Now that it's out in the open, now that you've said, *"Okay, have at it, you two"* he doesn't have to hide it anymore. For a lot of unfaithful spouses, hiding it has been half the fun. It's exciting, and it's often a big part of what fuels an extramarital affair and keeps that fantasy element going. That's true in almost all extramarital affairs, not just ones committed by men, and not just those that happen in midlife.

So I want you to think about this strategy if your husband refuses to end an affair. The pros are that it allows you to keep your personal power and dignity. It potentially deflates the forbidden excitement of his affair: when you step back, cold reality can descend more quickly on his hot romance. It doesn't feed your husband's ego. And very importantly, it sets a strong precedent in your marriage by showing your husband that you will never compete with another woman for something that should be yours already.

When He Wants to Have His Cake and Eat It, Too

I've already spoken about how a man who is going through a midlife crisis can be impulsive and unpredictable. He may not be sure about what he wants. One day it's you, the next it's her. One day he wants to work on the marriage, the next he wants a divorce.

The Shut-Out Wife

Other men who are going through a midlife episode are very certain what they want. They want freedom from their family or marital obligations, they want to move out and they want to be intimate with another woman—yet at the same time, they also want that safety net of their wife and marriage.

Perhaps they know, deep down, that their midlife episode is a passing phase, so they want to indulge in that and enjoy that to its fullest, but they don't want the drama of a messy divorce or having to tell their kids or having to divide up their assets.

Regardless, whether your husband doesn't know what he wants, or whether he knows full well what he wants, you may get mixed messages from him. And quite often, you will notice a fairly obnoxious development—one where he wants to have his cake and eat it, too.

I've seen this play out many times in practice. A female client will tell me that her midlife husband moved out of the home and is openly involved with another woman. Yet every now and then, maybe it's once and week or once a month, he'll come home and try to reconnect with her to some extent.

He may want to have sex. Or he may want her to cook him his favorite meal. Or he may want to use the garage or workshop facilities. Or he may want to use the laundry. Yet once he's fulfilled whatever need it was, he leaves again.

I call this the steak and sex syndrome, and I named it after speaking with a client whose husband was doing this exact thing. He had moved out and had a girlfriend. Yet every Sunday afternoon, he came home. His wife made him a steak and they had sex. Immediately afterward, he got up, took what he needed from the house—whether it was some fresh clothes or some coffee—and went back to his apartment.

And his wife was left in that emotional tailspin I've talked about so often, and that you've no doubt experienced. She was left to wonder what it all meant.

During dinner and during sex, she felt hopeful and connected. Did that mean he wanted her again? Did that mean he loved her and that he was ready to come back to her?

But then once the door closed behind him and she was left in the quiet house all alone, once again shut out of his life and left to clean up from supper and straighten the sheets, those feelings of hope and connection faded, and she was filled with feelings of sadness, disappointment and loss.

And every Sunday, from 5:00 pm to 8:00 pm, this little scenario would repeat itself.

Eventually, she came to realize what was happening. She was able to get control of that cycle of hope and disappointment and have some clarity. She came to realize that the whole thing was his way of keeping that safety net in his life.

This couple was quite well off financially and their kids were away at college, and her husband didn't want to upset the status quo. It would simply be too much of an inconvenience for him. It was much easier for him to just keep her on the line like this.

Not that he minded. She was a great cook and whenever they had sex she did her best to impress him. So really, it was a win-win for him. He got to have his cake and eat it, too. And all the while, he managed to keep total control over the situation.

Of course, since this man was in the full throes of a destructive, self-indulgent midlife episode, he gave little thought to what this might be doing to his wife. Because it really was ripping her heart out. It really was causing her to live in a constant state of uncertainty, anxiety and pain.

I always tell my clients to think long and hard about having sex with their husband if he's moved out of the home and especially if he's having sex with another woman. If he's moved out, you're not living as husband and wife—so it's perfectly reasonable that you would stop having sex.

Of course, you may want to continue. You may miss him terribly. You may long for the feel of his arms around you. You may desperately want to feel connected and reassured. You may see every chance to have sex as an opportunity to win him back.

If this is how you're thinking, you need to seriously challenge your thinking. Look at the facts. When you do have sex, does anything change? When you do let him have his cake and eat it too, does anything change?

I'm willing to bet not. Because when a person gets to have their cake and eat it, too, they have no motivation whatsoever to change. In fact, it's in their best interests to not change. Why would they? It doesn't get much better than that.

Time and time again, I've seen this dynamic eat away at a wife's emotional and physical well-being. If her husband is involved with another woman, there is definitely a health risk associated with being intimate with him.

On top of that, how do you feel when you do this? Do you feel good or confident or empowered? Do you feel loved and respected by him? Do you feel in control of your own life?

Now, it's absolutely true that some men (and women) who experience a serious midlife episode, or so-called midlife crisis, really don't know what they want. Some act in self-destructive and unhealthy ways, and some require the care of a mental health professional to help them with depression and so on.

But not all men. Many, if not most, continue to act in their best interests when it comes right down to it. They may be confused and uncertain about some things, but they can also have remarkable clarity when it comes to other things—usually things that have the potential to cost them money or cause them some kind of inconvenience or embarrassment. When it comes to things that affect their pocket book or their personal pleasure, they often know exactly what they want and what they are doing.

So I encourage you to have clarity, too. Push the pause button on your emotions and look at the situation from a distance. Does it look like your husband is trying to have his cake and eat it, too?

Look at the situation objectively. If this were all happening to your best friend or you sister, if their husband were acting like this, how would you interpret his behavior or motivations? What advice would you give your friend or sister? Give it some thought. Maybe it's time to take your own advice.

Circle the Date

Most of us have been told that ultimatums are a bad thing. They usually are. After all, if you have to threaten someone to do what you want, then they don't really want to do it. And that has a way of backfiring on you.

Yet ultimatums have their place. Back in part two, you read about a woman whose husband was in that "I don't know what I want" zone. If you'll remember, she put a deadline on his indecision, a deadline that was, for all intents and purposes in that situation, an ultimatum. She told him that he had to commit to their marriage within two weeks, or she would file for divorce.

Here's why that worked for her: because she meant it. Because she really was okay with whatever he chose to do. Had he continued to say he didn't know what he wanted, or had he continued to look at dating sites and give her attitude, she was totally prepared to begin the divorce process. She wasn't issuing the ultimatum from a position of powerlessness. She wasn't threatening or pressuring him, she was simply informing him of how it was going to be so that she could get on with her life either way.

If your husband is having an affair, no doubt you are also eager to get on with your life.

Should you issue an ultimatum? *"End your affair by the weekend or we're over for good?"* You can, but I tend to advise against it. I've seen too many cases where a woman felt strong and certain about doing this in the moment, but within a few hours, or perhaps a day or two, she regretted issuing the ultimatum. She just wasn't there yet.

And the last thing you want to do is issue an ultimatum and then not follow through.

That's why circling the date—and keeping it to yourself—might be a safer way to go. Choose a date when you're prepared to make a change in your life. It could be filing for divorce, but it doesn't have to be.

It could be selling your house or taking a job in a new city (do consult with a lawyer before making any big changes like this). Regardless, on that date, something is going to change.

Circling the actual date that you're prepared to make some kind of positive change in your life can give you a sense of control and certainty. You might not be able to know or control everything, but you do know that come that circled date on your hummingbird calendar, you're going to make a change. It's your personal choice. It's your little secret. It's the date of your clean break or your fresh start.

The thing is, human beings aren't good at living in a place of uncertainty, and we're especially not good at waiting for someone else's decision. If your husband has shut you out of his life, you're definitely living in that place—you may feel like all you're doing is waiting. Waiting for him to make a decision. Waiting for him to come back to you. You're stuck in that waiting room of life and it sucks.

Circling a date when you're prepared to make a change, something big, something with forward momentum, can help counteract that feeling of always waiting, waiting, waiting.

His Beck, Your Call

When a man's midlife episode escalates, he can become self-focused, self-indulgent, unpredictable and distant. He may send mixed messages. He effectively shuts out his wife from his life, creating a situation where she is left in a chronic state of speculation, anxiety and heartache. As a consequence, she may analyze his every word and action, looking for trace evidence that he still loves her and may open his life to her again. She lives to see and feel some kind of reassurance from him. Because of this, she may allow herself to be at his beck and call. Her phone is never more than an arm's length away so that she can instantly answer if he calls. If he sends her a text message while she's driving, she quickly pulls over to text him back. If he leaves a voicemail while she's at the movies, she steps out of the theater to call him back. If she had plans with friends, even big plans, she'll break them in an instant.

On top of that, she does everything she can to try to remain a central or meaningful figure in his life. She'll remind him of his dentist appointment or his mother's birthday. She'll do everything she can to constantly inject herself into his life. It's as though she's constantly trying to remind him that she's important or valuable.

Not all wives do this, but many do, and it's understandable. We all cling to what is slipping away. But like so many instinctual ways of behaving in a crisis, it can backfire. Think of a fire drill—you're told to walk, not run, even though your instinct is to run, right? That's because you have a better chance of getting through it by proceeding in a thoughtful, planned-out way. That's also the case when it comes to your husband's self-focused midlife episode.

When I talk to wives who are doing this—that is, remaining at their husband's "beck and call"—they often say the same thing:

"I'm afraid that he'll forget about me if I don't constantly remind him that I exist or that I'm useful. I'm afraid that if I don't instantly answer his call or text that I'll miss my opportunity. He might forget about me and never reach out again."

I hope reading this makes you realize just how unrealistic this way of thinking is. I get it. I understand the fear. But it's an unwarranted fear. *Your husband will not forget you exist.* Whatever else he does or doesn't do, whatever choices he makes, he will not forget you exist. He will not forget that you are an option that he can return to or embrace. He knows it. You don't need to remind him. And you certainly do not need to be at his beck and call. In fact, I strongly suggest you think about taking a different approach.

Do not be so accessible. Do not position yourself as someone who has nothing else to do but wait for and respond to any message he puts out there.

The truth is, many midlife men fully expect that their wife will be there whenever and however they want her to be. They expect that when they text or call, she'll answer. They expect her to be available whenever, wherever, however.

So I suggest that you think about challenging that expectation. Don't reply to his texts. He'll call if he wants to talk to you. If he calls, let it go to voicemail. Let him wonder what you're doing for a change. Let him wait for you for a change.

I often recommend this strategy to wives, and it's one that is as much about liberating you from that constant, agonizing state of uncertainty and expectation as anything else. I don't want you to be constantly waiting for some kind of sign from him.

There's one thing you need to accept—if he wants to see you, he will see you. And sometimes the more effort he has to put into that, the better. The thrill of the hunt, remember? Keep that ancient wisdom in mind.

All right. At this point, I want to walk you through a very typical scenario, one that often plays out when a woman implements this very strategy.

Her husband, who is having an affair and has moved out of the home, sends her a text message. He is asking for something insignificant—let's say he wants to know if she knows where his golf clubs are.

The Shut-Out Wife

Despite her desire to instantly reply to his text, his wife does not. Instead, she goes about her day. An hour later, her husband sends another text, asking why she hasn't replied to his first text. Again, she does not reply—after all, she is busy with other things, and this is not an urgent matter. A short time later, she receives a third text. This one is angrier. More indignant. More demanding—*Why haven't you replied?!*

Soon—and typically very soon, as in an hour or two—she finds that his efforts to reach her have gone up. Now, he calls. In addition to multiple texts, he leaves multiple voicemails, each more irritated and insulted that she isn't at his beck and call.

"I've been texting you all morning, why haven't you replied? This is my third voicemail. What are you doing?"

By the way, you'll notice his question—*What are you doing?* Depending on the circumstances, this might be the first time this husband hasn't been able to reach his wife, or doesn't know where she is, or what she's doing, or who she's doing it with, or when she might be back to answer his questions. He will want to know.

Now, if she continues to ignore him, or if she merely responds by saying, *"Sorry, I have a lot on the go. I don't know where your golf clubs are"* what she'll often find is that he either continues to be irritated and insulted—how dare you not reply to *me* right away!—or he'll start to show more interest in her life. In *her*.

Why? Because, more than likely, he feels his power and his control over the situation slipping away. Because his wife isn't playing the role he needs her and expects her to play. And he doesn't like it. It doesn't work for him. He needs her to be subordinate. He needs her to always be there for him. But when this woman steps back and looks at the situation more objectively, she may find that isn't what she needs.

So remember: it's his beck, but it's your call. That is an empowering thing to remember, and I hope you'll take it to heart.

The Shut-Out Wife's Creed

When a husband begins to show signs of having a midlife episode, it's important that his wife supports him and shows him that she cares about and respects his feelings, perspectives, grievances and so on. That's what part one of this book is all about. That's only fair. But if things continue to escalate to the point that he shuts her out and begins to treat her poorly, she needs to be aware of what is happening, and she needs to avoid falling into those knee-jerk, self-sabotaging behaviors: engaging in pointless arguments, repeating herself, constantly or excessively explaining herself, living only for him, challenging or insulting him, competing with another woman for him, inadvertently feeding his self-focus, and so on.

She needs to have clarity so that she can see his behavior for what it is. When he sends mixed messages, when he blames her for everything, when he re-writes the marital history, etc.—those may be his way of keeping control of the situation and of writing a narrative that suits his purposes and preferences.

When we step back and look at it, we can see that this requires a woman to take back her personal power—that is, she needs to empower herself in a healthy way, one that is respectful to her, her husband, and the marriage. It all aligns with the Fair, but Aware approach I talked about earlier.

But perhaps most important of all, a shut-out wife has to take care of herself while, at the same time, responding to his choices and behavior in a way that—despite everything—keeps the door open, so that at some point he may open it and ask her, with love and humility, to come back into his life.

To that end, I want to talk about the three D's: Disconnect, Distance, and Defamiliarize. These comprise the three parts of the shut-out wife's creed. Learn them. Live them.

These strategies, especially when used together, are powerful tools that can help you do what needs to be done. They also bring together many of the insights and ideas that I've covered in this book. Disconnect, distance and defamiliarize. I'll talk about each of them in turn.

First, Disconnect. You've learned a lot in this book. I hope you've gained clarity into your husband's words and actions. At this point you should have a good idea of whether, when and how you're being manipulated, so I want you to emotionally disconnect or detach from those manipulations. Actually visualize yourself disconnecting from them, as if you were disconnecting the phone line or pulling a plug out of a socket. I also want you to emotionally disconnect from your husband's behaviors and choices in a larger sense. If he's moved out, if he's having an affair—those things are his choices. They reflect upon him, not you.

When we're emotionally disconnected from something, we have clarity and self-control. There's a reason that surgeons are not allowed to operate on family—because they lose the ability to think clearly or act with skill or purpose. That's why a surgeon who is emotionally detached from the person on their operating table can actually do the best job for that person.

So emotional disconnection, detachment, can be a good thing. It can protect you. It can empower you. It doesn't mean you don't love your husband, it doesn't mean you don't care about him or your marriage or that you aren't open at some point to plugging back into each other.

Rather, it means that you are not going to let your emotions take over when you feel you're being manipulated or mistreated. It means that you're not going to become emotionally mired in whatever confused, mean, hurtful or conflicting emotions he's throwing your way.

Second, Distance. Let's say you're walking through the park when somebody points to a metal object a few feet away from you and says, *"That's a bomb!"* What do you do? Do you go toward it? Of course not. You get away from it, fast. Because it has the potential to hurt you very badly.

It's the same thing with a spouse's hurtful midlife episode. If you've done everything you can to help him, to support him, to acknowledge your part in any conflict and to encourage him to work on the marriage, but he still continues to hurt you—well, it's probably time to put some distance between you and him. If you can't safely defuse a bomb, you need to move away from it.

Of course, this is usually the opposite of what wives do. They don't run away from that destruction, they often run toward it. They throw themselves on top of it. They cling to it, even when everyone around them is saying, *"Hey, woman, that thing could go off any second—let go and step away!"*

In practice, putting distance between you and your husband does involve a degree of emotional disconnection or detachment, but it also involves a physical detachment, kind of like what I talked about in the previous section—not always being there for him.

Don't trip over yourself trying to return his text messages or phone calls. Don't wait around for him or break plans on the off-chance he might show up or want to see you. Don't act as his personal secretary or counselor.

Put some distance between the two of you. Not only will you protect yourself, but you'll be able to see things more clearly at that distance. So that's disconnect and distance.

The third D of the shut-out wife's creed is Defamiliarize. Defamiliarization is an artistic device, one that I often advise my clients to consider. At its most basic, it involves presenting something that is very familiar—whether that's a person or an object—in a new and unfamiliar way. It's about making someone do a double-take and say, *"Hey, that looks different"* or *"Hey, that isn't what I was expecting to see, or to have happen."*

Defamiliarization can be a very useful and effective strategy for a wife to use during her husband's midlife crisis, and it can be used in many different ways.

A spouse who is going through a midlife episode, especially one involving another woman, can be a very self-focused, self-indulgent person. He will often expect his wife to be at his beck and call. He will expect her to react and behave in certain ways. He will expect her to always be there, always predictable and familiar. In fact, he needs her to be like that. He needs her to be the dock that he can always sail back to if the waters get too rough.

That's why it can be effective to challenge his expectations and to make him (and yourself!) realize that you're not as predictable or familiar as he thinks you are. This can make you feel empowered, while making him start to realize that he doesn't hold all the power here. You are your own person, and that person is more than the wife he thinks he knows so well.

I've had clients utilize this strategy in many different ways. I remember one woman who used to do everything she could to keep her husband on the phone when he called (by the way, both women and men do this *all the time* when worried about their relationships, so don't be hard on yourself if it sounds familiar!). She'd keep asking questions, keep talking about pointless or trivial things—just hanging on his every word to the point that he would be really tired of the conversation and basically hang up on her. I encouraged her to defamiliarize this all too familiar interaction between them by a) having something really interesting or amusing ready to talk about in advance and b) ending the conversation pleasantly and promptly. She did, and within a few days, her husband was calling her more often.

I've also had clients who re-designed their homes when their husband moved out, or painted the interior a different color. They thought *"Hey, why should he be the only one who gets to change? Why should he be the only one who gets to re-create themselves? Maybe I should be doing that, too."*

The Shut-Out Wife

That kind of visual change can have quite the impact. When a husband who has moved out comes back to the home for whatever reason, he's met with an unexpected sight—the house looks different...somewhat unfamiliar.

And that sends him a strong message. You're not the only one capable of making changes. You're not the only one who's making choices and living your life. Even though you're not here, my life is still going on. I'm still doing things, I'm still experiencing things, I'm still moving forward. It's not all about you.

Other clients have made physical changes to their appearance. They've colored their hair, got a new style or let it grow out. They've updated their make-up style. They've also updated or changed the style of clothes they wear. And they often have a lot of fun doing this. When you look in the mirror and see these changes, it can be very liberating and empowering.

And again, this can send a strong message to your husband. My life is moving forward without you. Despite your choices and words and actions, I have not curled up into a little ball and given up. I'm doing fine. In fact, I'm doing a lot better than you probably expected I would.

So as you can see, combining these strategies—disconnect, distance and defamiliarize—is a good way to protect yourself while also letting your husband know that it isn't all about him.

Here's an example of all three working together. Let's say your husband texts you this message "I need to come by the house on Friday and pick up my dress shoes."

Let me ask you: are you going to obsess about why he needs his dress shoes? No. Are you going to analyze his text and cry over it? No. Are you going to break the plans you had with your friends, and immediately text him back by saying, *"Sure, come by anytime on Friday, I'm around all day. Do you want to stay for supper? I can cook a steak."* No. Are you going to clean up the house and make sure everything is just the way he likes it, so he feels all warm and cozy? No.

Instead, you're going to ignore the text for a while, and you're going to ignore all the other texts he sends, the ones where he becomes increasingly irritated because you aren't immediately responding to him.

Instead, you're going to wait for him to call and leave you a voicemail...which he will. And when he does, he is going to hear your new voicemail greeting. This in itself will be unfamiliar to him. He won't be expecting it.

After he leaves a voicemail, you can text him back. Keep it short, civil and casual: *"I don't know if I'll be around on Friday, but I'll leave your shoes on the back step."*

What is your husband's takeaway from all this? His takeaway is that you're not obsessing about him. You're not always going to be there for him. You're living your life, moving forward, not spinning your wheels waiting with bated breath for him to call you. You cannot be manipulated and you won't continue to do nothing but wait around for him while he disrespects you or shuts you out. You're making your own changes, and he has no control over that. And that, in a nutshell, is how the three D's—disconnect, distance, defamiliarize—of the shut-out wife's creed can work, and work in your best interests.

How Will He React?

In the previous section I talked about using the shut-out wife's creed (the three D's) to, among other things, protect yourself and send your husband the message that you have control over your life. How might a husband react to all of this? He may react positively and change for the better.

Or he may react negatively, at least initially, because he doesn't like what is happening. People (that includes him, you and me) don't like it when someone doesn't do what we want, or when they don't make something easy for us.

So when you emotionally disconnect, when you put distance between you and your husband, when you defamiliarize what he expects to be familiar and unchanged, don't be surprised if you see a reaction from him.

In many cases, these changes will make a man wonder—*"Hey, am I losing control of this a bit?"* And if he feels that way, he may react by trying to regain that control.

How? That's a big question, and there are different answers depending on the person and their personality. Some men will try to intimidate their spouse through anger or accusation. Others may pretend they don't notice (they do). Others may become increasingly cool or distant, while still others will do the opposite—they may try to cozy up to their wife.

The same husband may at different times try all of these things, depending on the results he gets.

Regardless, the purpose is often the same. First, it's to determine just how serious his wife is about all of this. Second, it's to disarm her and regain control of the situation as much as possible.

Let's say for example that you change something about the house…maybe you paint the kitchen. When he sees this, he might say, *"Oh, so you're moving on without me…well, I guess our marriage really is over then."*

The tactic here is to turn it around and scare you, so that you panic and say, *"Oh, no, I just painted the kitchen because it needed it…our marriage isn't over!"* See? Now he knows you weren't that serious, and he's back in control. You've lost ground and he's gained it back.

Or, he might do the opposite.

He might walk in, see the kitchen and tear up. He might say, *"This is so hurtful…it's clear you're moving on without me."* The tactic here is to tap into your compassion and make you feel sorry for him, so that you react by saying, *"Don't cry…I'm not moving on without you, I could never do that!"* See? Now he's back in control. You've lost ground and he's gained it back.

* * * * * *

FROM DON'S DESK

One of the most common ways a woman "defamiliarizes" herself is by changing her appearance. I'm mention this because commenting on this is also one of the most common ways a guy will try to make a woman feel self-conscious.

Let's say you change your hairstyle. He might see it and say, *"Oh, so you're trying to win me back by looking better?"* He'll make you try to feel bad or foolish, implying that you're only changing yourself for him.

If he does this, don't react by saying, *"No, I'm doing it for me!"* If you do that, he will know that he's gotten to you. Just shrug it off and walk away.

If he sees your new hair, he might also accuse you of looking for a new man already. *"What's with the new hair? Are you out on the prowl already?"* Don't take this bait. Shrug it off.

He wants you to stay unchanged and familiar. When you don't do that, he feels his power slipping away. And if you've changed your appearance, he knows he can get to you by pointing it out in some petty way and making you feel self-conscious about it.

Here's the good news. He notices that you look good, even better, and that's hard to stomach. He'd much prefer you to look like a unwashed vagabond living in the despair of his absence.

* * * * * * *

If you feel the three D's strategy is suitable and you want to try it, here's another thing to keep in mind. Don't put too much stock in your husband's initial reaction, whether it's good or bad.

This is what I mean: I was working with a shut-out wife who decided to try this three-part strategy—disconnect, distance and defamiliarize—and almost immediately her husband seemed to have a change of heart. He seemed to snap out of his midlife episode.

As soon as she stopped instantly responding to his texts and basically structuring her life around his, he sensed that she was empowering herself and likely reaching her breaking point with his self-focused behavior and infidelity.

So he came rushing back home. He told her that he'd been selfish and short-sighted. He told her that he had ended his affair with the other woman and that he wanted nothing more than to earn her forgiveness and love back. He told her that the whole thing had made him realize just how much he loved her and couldn't live without her. It was everything my client wanted to hear.

But instead of being cautious and taking things slowly, just to make sure he was being completely authentic, she couldn't help herself. She had just been waiting too long to hear those words from him. Consequently, she immediately fell back into his arms and had sex with him.

Afterward, as they were lying in bed and she was basking in the afterglow of reconnecting with her husband, she felt the change—and right before her eyes, he began to backtrack.

All of a sudden, he wasn't quite sure what he wanted. Maybe they'd made a mistake, he said.

He told her that their lovemaking just had not stirred in him the feelings or passion that he thought it would.

And then he got out of bed and left.

You can imagine the state this woman was left in. I do not want that to happen to you. Therefore, I urge you to not put too much stock into his reaction, whether that reaction is good or bad. If his reaction is good and he suddenly wants you back, don't let your hope and love for him make you blind to what might be happening. It might be a tactic. He may have no intentions of ending his affair, at least not right now.

If his reaction is bad, say he threatens divorce, don't let your fear back you into a corner. It too might be a tactic. He may have no intentions of filing for divorce. And by the way, don't let the word "divorce" rattle you too much. It ain't over 'til it's over. Many people have started divorce proceedings but ended them to reconcile. I've even had clients reconcile and re-marry after divorce. I can't guarantee that will happen for you—there are no guarantees with any of this—but I can tell you that it happens.

Your takeaway from this is to cool your heels. Think clearly and use common sense. If something is working, keep doing it. You already know this, don't you? I mean, if you used a certain strategy and it helped you get healthier or save more money you'd keep using it, right? Right. So do that here.

How long should you stick to your strategy? I can't answer that. Only you can be the judge of that. I would encourage you, however, to put more stock into your husband's actions than in whatever he says to you. Actions always speak louder than words. I often remind my clients of this simple little rule—when the words and the actions don't match, believe the actions.

Stick to your guns and see what he does. Does he end the affair and offer you proof of that? Does he show true humility and insight into his own behavior? Is he honest and fully accountable for what he's done? Does he acknowledge the impact his words and behaviors have had on you? Has he taken steps to get professional help, if he requires it? Is he patient enough to prove to you that he truly wants to recommit to you and to your marriage?

Or, does he expect you to instantly take him at his word, despite everything that has happened? Is he still defending or downplaying his behavior? Does he still show traces of that confusion or uncertainty? Does he still send mixed messages? Does he still guard his cell phone or get impatient when you ask him a question? Does he still show signs that it's all about him?

Because if he slips up and shows these kinds of signs, then I'm sorry, but nothing has changed.

Talk to the Man You Married

Easier said than done. I've expressed that sentiment repeatedly in this book. That's because I'm well aware that many of the insights and strategies herein seem straightforward enough when you read them, but when you find yourself face to face with a person who is being difficult, it's not quite so easy to put them into practice.

Yet I can suggest an easy-to-remember, easy-to-use tip that can be enormously helpful when you find yourself face to face with your husband's challenging behavior—a mixed message, confusion, anger, meanness, accusation, etc.—or even when you hear a baffling statement from him.

Here is that tip: No matter what he says or does, no matter how foreign or inaccessible he seems to you, always talk to the man you married. Because he's in there.

Yes, he might be buried under a lot of self-focus, resentment, confusion, frustration, even ego,...but he's still in there.

Even it seems like he doesn't hear you, he does. Even if he isn't listening at the time you say the words, he will remember your words. And at some point, when he is alone and reflective, he will give them some thought.

Therefore, always talk to the man you married.

Talk to him with imaginary blinders on, if you must. Ignore his harsh voice tone, his words, his facial expressions, and talk to the man who was once loving to you, and who you once felt very secure and comfortable with. Talk right through the curtain of his unpleasant midlife behavior and speak directly to the man behind it.

By this, I do *not* mean to speak to him in an overly supportive or soft way, or in a pleading or emotional way.

What I *do* mean, is to speak to him with confidence, knowing that he is an adult man who is capable of hearing you, of understanding you, just as he used to.

Do Men Usually Go Back to Their Wives? Do They "Snap Out of It?"

Whenever I'm consulting with a woman whose husband is going through a self-focused midlife episode, and particularly one where he has been or is being unfaithful, I know she's going to ask me this question: *"Do men usually go back to their wives? Do they usually snap out of it, come to their senses and recommit to their marriage?"*

The short answer is yes. In my experience, the excitement of an extramarital affair does wear thin—the more time he spends with the other woman, the more likely he is to realize she isn't "all that." That process happens in almost all affairs, not just ones that happen during a midlife crisis.

At the same time, the fantasy life that he's created for himself will also most likely wear off. Fantasies always give way to reality.

But how long it will take for that to happen remains to be seen. And whether or not your particular husband will choose to recommit to the marriage—truly recommit, heart and soul—remains to be seen. Because ultimately, if he does come back to you, it has to be his choice. He has to want it. He has to want it more than anything, he has to want it with his whole heart and soul.

In the end, whether a man comes back after a destructive midlife crisis may also depend on his personality and character. Some men, some people in general, are more stubborn than others. They won't admit when they've made a mistake. They have too much pride. They won't admit when they're wrong and they won't be accountable or apologize for the ways they've hurt others, even those they care about.

The unhappy truth is that many men who have the kind of self-focused midlife episode that escalates to the point of infidelity have this type of personality to begin with. Many wives have told me there was evidence of this earlier in the marriage—previous infidelities, and a trend of self-indulgent or narcissistic behavior.

If your husband is not typically like this, if he has not previously shown signs of being a self-focused person, then your marriage may have better odds of surviving, and of actually going on to become happy and fulfilling for both of you again.

One thing I can tell you with absolute certainty, however, is that if he does come back, he will remember how you responded to his words and behavior while he was in the throes of his midlife episode. If you showed strength, if you kept your dignity, if you kept your personal power while respecting his and him, and if you stayed in control over your own life—he will remember that.

And that will have a direct bearing on how he feels and thinks about you.

It will also have a direct bearing on his future choices. He must know that if he treats you like this again, if he disrespects your marriage like this again, you will be gone. He must know that you won't put yourself through it a second time.

That's more important than you know.

Because I sometimes hear from women who say that even though their husband came back after his midlife crisis, he never really came back. He was always changed. That streak of self-indulgence and the behavior that goes with it never really went away.

I think that often happens in cases where the wife begged him to come back, lived her life around him, or competed with other women for him. He might come back, but as far as he's concerned, it's on his terms. And unfortunately, that's just a part of human nature. We all tend to do what we can get away with.

That's why I've encouraged you, again and again, to respect him while respecting yourself. To act supportively and honestly, but also to act in your own best interests. Because if you don't, who will? Always be fair, but aware.

Q&A's, Part Three

<u>The Midlife Man & Other (Younger) Women</u>

If your spouse's brief glances at pretty women become too blatant or hurtful to you, how will you respond?

<u>What to Do When He Strikes Up a Close "Friendship"
with Another Woman</u>

What is your deepest fear about the other woman's desirability? How might your fear-based assumptions be skewing the way you think about her?

Write down the things you should **not** do when it comes to the "other woman".

How might "depersonalizing" this other woman/friend help you regain your power, dignity and sense of self-worth?

If your husband is involved with another woman, might withdrawing emotional and sexual intimacy help you maintain your dignity and well-being? Why or why not?

If you withdraw emotional and sexual intimacy while he is involved with another woman, what message does that send him about you?

How might your husband react if you withdraw emotional or sexual intimacy? Why might he react this way?

How will you handle his reaction?

<u>How to Know If He's Having an Affair</u>

What makes you suspect or believe that your husband is having an affair?

Do you have proof or an admission from him that he is having an affair? If not, are you confident in your own assessment of the situation, based on your knowledge of your husband (i.e. his habits, behaviors, etc.) and of your own marriage?

How has your husband responded to questions about an affair or this other woman? Did his responses reassure you? How did they make you feel?

When He Wants to Move Out and Get His Own Place

If he says he wants to move out, how can you respond in a way that he won't be expecting? How can you respond in a way that makes him realize you have a say, too?

Although is a sad and scary thing, might there be any benefit to his moving out? Might something positive potentially come out of it? Write down your thoughts about this.

If he says he is going to move out, how will you respond? What should you **not** do?

If he does actually move out, how will you respond? What should you **not** do?

When He's Unfaithful

How will you practice good self-care if you discover he has been unfaithful? How will you maintain your perspective, dignity, power and well-being? Think about this and answer in detail.

Do you feel that you are doing "all the work" to save the marriage, even though he is the unfaithful one? Has that worked to your benefit or motivated him to step up?

If you were to stop doing all the work, what message might that send to your spouse? What change might that (eventually) prompt in him?

Do some soul-searching—is infidelity a deal-breaker for you? Why or why not?

You are here to save your marriage, if that is possible; however, what long-term effects might your husband's affair have on you, as a woman, even if he does recommit to you?

When He Won't End His Affair

Do you feel you are possibly in a "love triangle" situation? Why or why not?

How might a "love triangle" make your husband feel about and perceive himself? Is that a situation he will want to end?

Do you feel that you are or must compete with his affair partner? If you compete with this other woman for him, how might that affect your well-being, self-perception and sense of personal empowerment?

If you compete with this other woman for your husband, how might that affect his perception of you and the way he feels about you?

If you compete with this other woman for him, what "precedent" (if any) might that set in your marriage?

The Oldest Relationship Advice in the World

Yes, it's the 21st century, but might this ancient piece of relationship advice—Don't chase boys!—be useful in your situation?

If you believe this may be useful in some way, write down those ways.

If you are hesitant to use this kind of strategy, why is that?

How to Motivate Him to End His Affair

What do you suspect is motivating your spouse to continue on with the affair?

How might refusing to compete for him and stepping away from the situation, thus allowing the love triangle to collapse, affect the dynamics of the relationship between your husband and the other woman?

How might doing the opposite of what he expects—giving him to the other woman instead of trying to wrestle him away from her—affect how your husband sees you? How might it affect how he sees the affair, the other woman or even himself?

Think about that dynamic, and write down your thoughts in detail.

When He Wants to Have His Cake and Eat It, Too

Do you feel that your husband wants to "have his cake and eat it, too"? If so, how?

How does this affect you? Do you ever find yourself trapped in that cycle of hope and despair? Think about this and be specific.

If he has moved out of the home, do you feel that continuing to have sex with him is leading him to re-commit to you (i.e. Has he left the other woman?)

How do you feel about yourself when / after you have sex with him (assuming he is involved with another person at this time)?

Circle the Date

Might circling a date help you move forward? If so, what change will you make on that date, and how might it help you?

What date will you circle? Are there are any steps you should take to prepare before the circled date arrives?

Are you truly ready to circle that date? Why or why not?

His Beck, Your Call

Are you "always there" for your husband? If so, what does that make him think or feel about you? How does that affect his motivation to change?

If you are not so accessible or "always there" for him—how might that affect the way he thinks or feels about you?

How might your husband react when you realizes you are no longer "always there" for him?

If he reacts in a negative way, how will you deal with that?

The Shut-Out Wife's Creed

How can you emotionally disconnect or detach from him and the situation? How might that benefit or protect you?

How can you get distance from his hurtful behavior or words, or the situation itself? How might that benefit or protect you?

How can you defamiliarize your responses, behaviors, appearance, etc.? How might that benefit or protect you?

Might defamiliarizing yourself and your life actually inspire you and make you feel better? How so?

Replay! Think back to an interaction between you and your husband, one that you felt went poorly. Now replay that, incorporating what you've learned so far—might you have been able to handle yourself, and the situation, better or differently?

How Will He React?

How might your husband react when he sees you taking back your personal power? Why might he react in these ways and how will you respond to him?

If your husband says he wants to re-commit to you and the marriage, how can you be certain that he is being sincere? What evidence have you seen that he is sincere?

Talk to the Man You Married

Think back. Has there been an interaction between you and your spouse where this tip—talk to the man you married—might have helped you keep your cool or get through it?

Imagine yourself having an interaction with your spouse and using this tip in action: even speak aloud, so you are accustomed to using the kind of words or language you might use when you use this tip.

Do Men Usually Go Back to Their Wives?
Do They "Snap Out of It?"

Has your spouse shown this kind of behavior—self-focus, untrustworthiness, etc.—earlier in the relationship or marriage?

Further to the above question, how do you think that may influence or predict how he chooses to behave now?

How might your behavior affect your husband's behavior, now and in the future?

In Closing:

The Meaning of (Mid)Life

The 50/50

As we come to end of this book, there's something else I feel compelled to mention…although part of me is hesitant to mention it, for the very reason that I feel compelled to mention it! I call it the 50/50. Right around middle age (and for the record, I'm on the dark side of middle age at the time of writing), it seems to me, both professionally and personally, that a woman reaches a crossroads in her life. I think this applies to almost all of women, regardless of whether they are in happy marriages, unhappy marriages, divorced, widowed, or never married. At this crossroads, she has to make a conscious choice of how to live the rest of her life.

There's a fifty percent chance she will choose to live it with as much joy, perspective, and positivity as possible. She will care for herself, learn to accept the slings and arrows of life's injustices, and be grateful for the good things in her life. She will choose to smile, knowing that, when you smile, the world smiles with you, and she wants to be part of the world.

There's also a fifty percent chance that she'll choose to live it in misery and resentment. She'll dwell on those injustices and let them define her. She will descend into negativity, interpreting everything around her in a bad light. And eventually, she'll create her own reality, as people pull away from her—that, or she only draws to her people who are just as negative.

I don't mean to make light of what you are going through, but I also know that you've gone through many struggles in your life, and you're still here. You're still kicking. You're still a force to be reckoned with, even if you've forgotten that a little bit.

I've faced the 50/50 crossroads, and I know many other women who have, too. When you find yourself there—if you do—I hope you will remember that there is more to your life, your worth, and your story, than this one experience. It does not define you or your life, and it should not determine how you, as an individual woman, choose to live the rest of your life.

The Part You're Given

And speaking of your story... I'm reminded of an experience I had back in university. A friend asked me to stand in last minute in a play she had written after her regular actress bailed. I had no talent for the stage, but it was a one-liner part, so I did it as a favor.

The whole experience made me realize something about the theatre. Most of the drama happens behind the scenes. There was one girl in particular who didn't want to play a certain role, and right until the moment the curtain rose, she kept saying, "I don't want to play this part!"

The performance ended up going well, but for years afterward, whenever I or my friend found ourselves stuck having to do something we didn't really want to do, we'd cry out, "I don't want to play this part!" It was our funny little battle cry.

Because there are definitely times in life that we're given a certain part to play. That's not always a bad thing—indeed, we are eager to receive some of these parts—and not all of them are difficult or unpleasant to play. Some of them just come with the territory of certain roles in life. A businesswoman has to play a certain part to maintain an aura of professionalism. A mother has to play a certain part to maintain a good relationship with her kids.

But there are also times when certain parts are thrust upon us. I guess one benefit of making it to midlife is that we begin to distinguish between the two. We get better at sticking around to play the parts we want and exiting stage left when we're given ones we don't want. We get better at distinguishing between which parts give our life meaning and which don't.

We especially learn that no one part is all meaningful. There is no one job, one relationship, one interest, one event, one success or one failure that encompasses us wholly. Our life has many parts and our life's meaning is greater than the sum of those parts.

Why am I going on about this?

Because I've found that *some* women who have been married for a very long time, and who have devoted a good portion of their life to their husband, lose sight of this. And if they're faced with their husband's midlife crisis at some point, their assumption—that the only part worth playing in life is that of his wife—can make a bad situation even worse.

This woman may worry that if the marriage ends, all those years she spent with her husband will be meaningless. She doesn't really know who she is without him. Her identity is very much wrapped up in the marriage. And that can make her even more fearful of the marriage ending. It can intensify her feelings of sadness or anxiety and make her act in ways that aren't in her best interests or the best interests of her marriage in the long run.

And a big reason for her fear-driven behavior is because she sees herself as being part of her husband's story, not the other way around.

She sees herself in a sort of supporting or co-starring role. He's the star of the show, and she's afraid to get fired.

If you've ever felt this way or in a way that's similar to this—that your identity or your story sort of hinges on your spouse and being married to him—I want you to try and turn that around a little bit.

Think about it like this: *"If this marriage ends and my husband leaves, that means he is no longer meant to be in my story. My story is moving on, going in a different direction, and it may not include him."*

For some women, this is a new way to look at it. It puts what is happening in your marriage in the larger context of your life—whatever happens, you will still be you.

You are the star of your own show and you play many meaningful parts in that show. Your life, your story, will go on. It will still have meaning and good times. It will still have laugher and surprises.

Now, of course, I hope your marriage will go on, too. This isn't meant to suggest that divorce is inevitable. Rather, this whole discussion is about you finding meaning in your life in different ways and knowing that nothing is inevitable (okay, there's that whole death and taxes thing, but other than that…)

If you're already doing this and this discussion is moot, great. Keep doing what you're doing.

But if any part of this resonates with you and you think, *"Maybe there's some truth to this,"* then just sit with it for some time and think.

Is your story, your life, big enough? Or is it time to write some new parts for yourself? Is it time to bring more meaning into your life in whatever ways are doable or interesting to you?

Of course you are afraid of losing your husband and marriage, but you need to face down that fear just like you've faced down a thousand other fears in your life. And one way to do that is to know that your life has meaning with or without him.

I want it to be *with* him, I really do. But the more you know that your life has meaning regardless, the more likely it is that you will find the strength and clarity to work through and emerge from this marriage crisis with a husband who loves and respects you more than ever.

So Now What?

We've covered a lot of ground in this book. You've come a long way. In part one, you learned some essential insights and strategies to help you avoid or downgrade your husband's midlife crisis.

In part two, you learned how to handle yourself, and the situation, when his midlife crisis escalates and when his behavior turns self-focused and self-serving.

Here in part three, you learned some important insights and ideas to help you navigate his friendships with other women, as well as extramarital affairs.

So now what? Well, now you let it all sink in for a while. I've included a massive amount of information in this book, but there is no one-size-fits-all approach when it comes to a spouse's self-indulgent midlife episode, and obviously a book like this cannot address the particulars of your specific situation.

That's why you need to go through this information carefully and decide what is right for you. I also recommend that you give it some time and read through this book again. Even skim it. You're in an emotional place, and sometimes people need to read things a couple of times before it really sinks in or makes sense. That's especially so with a book like this.

Similarly, if you found certain parts or sections of this book particularly useful, then you might want to occasionally revisit those to either stay focused or to refresh your memory.

Words of Wisdom

As this book draws to a close, I'd like to share with you a quote from Shakespeare (*A Midsummer Night's Dream*): "*And though she be but little, she is fierce.*"

This has become something of a mantra for many women and a way to express feminine strength. The character is small—we are all small, in this big world—and yet she is true to herself and manages to find happiness.

I know that you can do that, too, and I truly hope you've found content herein that might make that a little easier, even in some small way.

Everything I've suggested in this book stems from something I learned in practice, working with women who felt shut out of their husband's life during his midlife episode.

It also stems from what I learned from their husbands, both during and after the midlife episode.

Nonetheless, as I've already indicated, not everything will work for you. Not every insight will be relevant, not every strategy will be appropriate, and some of it you just might not care for. A book like this is general in nature, and I've provided what I feel is a broad spectrum of material for people to draw from.

What I can tell you for certain, however, is that I respect what you are going through and how difficult this time is for you. If you ever feel that you require more, different, or in-person help of any kind, please get it. Be proactive and find the right person for the job.

I will leave you with my very best wishes and hopes that, regardless of what happens in your marriage, you as an individual woman will live your life to the very fullest.

All best,
Debra Macleod